# Informational Passages
# for Text Marking & Close Reading

GRADE 5

By Marcia Miller & Martin Lee

NEW YORK • TORONTO • LONDON • AUCKLAND • SYDNEY
MEXICO CITY • NEW DELHI • HONG KONG • BUENOS AIRES

**Teaching** *Resources*

Cover design: Brian LaRossa
Interior design: Kathy Massaro

Photos ©: 14: yulyla/Fotolia; 16: abimages/Shutterstock, Inc.; 18: Aspen Photo/Shutterstock, Inc.;
22: Rob Marmion/Shutterstock, Inc.; 24: Ryan M. Bolton/Shutterstock, Inc.; 26: James Wilson/© Evelyn Glennie;
28: Hemmarat/Shutterstock, Inc.; 30: Blamb/Shutterstock, Inc.; 32: Stephen Rees/Shutterstock, Inc.; 34: The Granger Collection;
36: Edward S. Curtis/Library of Congress; 38: donatas1205/Shutterstock, Inc.; 40: ZU_09/iStockphoto; 42: Salma Arastu;
44: Nazzu/Shutterstock, Inc.; 46: Bettmann/Corbis Images; 48: Rick Bajornas/United Nations Photo;
50: tacar/Shutterstock, Inc.; 52: Bettmann/Corbis Images.

ISBN: 978-0-545-79381-0
Copyright © 2015 by Scholastic Inc.
All rights reserved.
Printed in the U.S.A.
Published by Scholastic Inc.

2  3  4  5  6  7  8  9  10        40      22  21  20  19  18  17  16

# Contents

### Informational Text Passages

## Main Idea & Details

## Sequence of Events

## Fact & Opinion

## Compare & Contrast

## Cause & Effect

## Context Clues

## Problem & Solution

## Summarize

## Make Inferences

## Author's Purpose

*Informational Passages for Text Marking & Close Reading: Grade 5*
© 2015 by Scholastic Teaching Resources

# Introduction

The vast majority of what adults read—in books, magazines, or online—is nonfiction. We read news stories, memoirs, science pieces, sports articles, business e-mails and memos, editorials, arts reviews, health documents, assembly or installation instructions, advertisements, and catalogs. Informational reading, with its diverse structures, formats, and content-specific vocabulary, can be demanding.

Many students enjoy reading nonfiction, but navigating the wide variety of rich informational texts poses challenges for evolving readers. Students may lack sufficient background knowledge of a topic or be unfamiliar with specific vocabulary related to it. In addition, they may find some structures or features of nonfiction puzzling. This is why exposing students more frequently to complex informational texts and introducing them to active reading-comprehension strategies are now key components of successful reading instruction. Useful strategies, clearly taught, can empower readers to approach informational texts purposefully, closely, and independently. Such active tools provide students with a foundation for success not only in school, but for the rest of their lives.

**Connections to the Standards**

The chart on page 9 details how the lessons in this book will help your students meet the more rigorous demands of today's reading standards for informational text.

## Text Marking: A Powerful Active-Reading Strategy

To improve their comprehension of complex informational texts, students must actively engage with the text. Careful and consistent text marking by hand is one valuable way to accomplish that. To begin with, by numbering paragraphs, students can readily identify the location of pertinent information when discussing a piece. By circling main ideas, underlining supporting details (such as definitions, descriptions, evidence, explanations, and data), and boxing key vocabulary, students interact directly with the material, making it more digestible in the process. But the true goal of teaching text marking is to help students internalize an effective close-reading strategy, not to have them show how many marks they can make on a page.

Purposeful text marking intensifies a reader's focus. It helps readers identify information as they read and recognize and isolate key details or connect relevant ideas presented in the text. For instance, boxing words like *before, next, finally*, and *after* can clarify the sequence of ideas or events in a passage. By circling expressions like *I think* or *in my opinion*, students learn to discern opinions from facts. When students are asked to compare and contrast information in a passage, boxing signal words and phrases, such as *both, in the same way*, or *however*, can make identifying similarities and differences more apparent. Words like *since, because of, therefore*, or *as a result* signal cause-and-effect relationships that structure a piece. Furthermore, the physical act of writing by hand, in itself, helps students not only process what they read, but remember it as well.

*Informational Passages for Text Marking & Close Reading: Grade 5*
© 2015 by Scholastic Teaching Resources

## About the Passages

The 20 reproducible passages in this book, which vary in genres and forms, organizational structures, purposes, tones, and tasks, address ten key reading-comprehension skills, from identifying main ideas and details, and separating facts from opinions to summarizing and making inferences. Consult the table of contents to see the scope of skills, genres, forms, content areas, and Lexile scores of the passages. The Lexile scores fall within the ranges recommended for fifth graders. (The scores for grade 5, revised to reflect the more rigorous demands of today's higher standards, range from 830 to 1010.)

Each passage appears on its own page, beginning with the title, the genre or form of the passage, and the main comprehension skill the passage addresses. Most of the passages include visual elements, such as photographs, illustrations, or diagrams, as well as typical text elements, such as italics and captions.

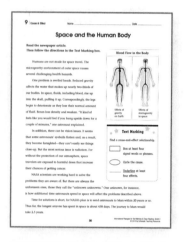

The passages are stand-alone texts and can be used in any order you choose. Feel free to assign passages to individuals, pairs, small groups, or the entire class, as best suits your teaching style. However, it's a good idea to preview each passage before you assign it, to ensure that your students have the skills needed to complete it successfully. (See the next page for a close-reading routine to model for students.)

## Reading-Comprehension Question Pages

Following each passage is a reproducible "Do More" page of text-dependent comprehension questions: two are multiple-choice questions that call for a single response and a brief, text-based explanation to justify that choice. The other two questions are open-response items. The questions address a range of comprehension strategies and skills. All questions share the goal of ensuring that students engage in close reading of the text, grasp its key ideas, and provide text-based evidence to support their answers. Have additional paper on hand so students have ample space to write complete and thorough answers.

An answer key (pages 54–63) includes annotated versions of each marked passage and sample answers to its related questions. Maintain flexibility in assessing student responses, as some markings and answers to open-response questions may vary. (Since students are likely to mark different places in the text as examples for particular skills, the annotated versions in the answer key highlight a variety of possible responses.) Encourage students to self-assess and revise their answers as you review the text markings together. This approach encourages discussion, comparison, extension, reinforcement, and correlation to other reading skills.

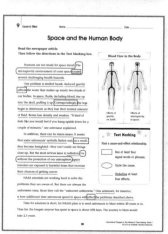

*Informational Passages for Text Marking & Close Reading: Grade 5*
© 2015 by Scholastic Teaching Resources

# Teaching Routine for Close Reading and Purposeful Text Marking

Any text can become more accessible to readers who have learned to bring various strategies, such as purposeful text marking, to the reading process. Here is one suggested routine that may be effective in your classroom.

## Preview

* **Engage prior knowledge** of the topic of the piece and its genre. Help students link it to similar topics or examples of the genre they may have read.

* **Identify the reading skill** for which students will be marking the text. Distribute the Comprehension Skill Summary Card that applies to the passage. Go over its key ideas. (See Comprehension Skill Summary Cards, page 8, for more.)

## Model *(for the first passage, to familiarize students with the process)*

* **Display the passage**, using an interactive whiteboard, document camera, or other resource, and provide students with their own copy. Preview the text with students by having them read the title and look at any photographs, illustrations, or other graphics.

* **Draw attention to the markings** students will use to enhance their understanding of the piece. Link the text marking box to the Comprehension Skill Summary Card for clarification.

* **Read aloud the passage** as students follow along. Guide students to think about the skill and to note any questions they may have on sticky-notes.

* **Mark the text together.** Begin by numbering the paragraphs. Then discuss the choices you make when marking the text, demonstrating and explaining how the various text elements support the skill. Check that students understand how to mark the text using the various icons and graphics shown in the text marking box.

## Read

* **Have students do a quick-read of the passage independently** for the gist. Then they should read it a second time, marking the text as they go.

* **Encourage students to make additional markings of their own.** These might include noting unfamiliar vocabulary, an idiom or phrase they may not understand, or an especially interesting, unusual, or important detail they want to remember. Invite them to use sticky-notes, colored pencils, highlighters, question marks, or check marks.

## Respond

* **Have students read the passage a third time.** This reading should prepare them to discuss the piece and offer their views about it.

* **Have students answer the questions** on the companion Do More page. Encourage them to look back at their text markings and other text evidence. This will help students provide complete and supported responses.

*Informational Passages for Text Marking & Close Reading: Grade 5*
© 2015 by Scholastic Teaching Resources

## Comprehension Skill Summary Cards

To help students review the ten reading-comprehension skills this book addresses and the specific terms associated with each, have them use the ten reproducible Comprehension Skill Summary Cards (pages 10–12). The boldface terms on each card are the same ones students will identify as they mark the text.

You might duplicate, cut out, and distribute a particular Comprehension Skill Summary Card before assigning a passage that focuses on that skill. Discuss the elements of the skill together to ensure that students fully grasp it. Encourage students to save and collect the cards, which they can use as a set of reading aids to refer to whenever they read any type of informational text.

### Tips and Suggestions

- The text-marking process is versatile and adaptable. Although numbering, boxing, circling, and underlining are the most common methods, you can personalize the strategy for your class if it helps augment the process. You might have students use letters to mark text; they can, for example, write MI to indicate a main idea, D to mark a detail, or F for fact and O for opinion. Whichever technique you use, focus on the need for consistency of marking.

- You may wish to extend the text-marking strategy by having students identify other aspects of writing, such as figurative language or confusing words, expressions, or idioms. Moreover, you can invite students to write their own notes and questions in the margins.

---

Comprehension Skill

### Main Idea & Details

Every passage has one or more main ideas supported by details. The main idea answers the question, "Who (or What) is this piece about?"

- The **main idea** is the most important point an author makes about a topic. The main idea in most paragraphs is stated in a *topic sentence*. The topic sentence can appear anywhere in a paragraph.

- **Supporting details** are facts, statements, examples, descriptions, and other information that tell more about the main idea.

---

Comprehension Skill

### Sequence of Events

As you read, notice the order in which things happen or ideas are presented. Think about the *beginning, middle,* and *end*.

- **Events** are the important actions that happen.

- The **sequence** is the order in which events happen.

- **Signal words** give clues that help clarify the order of events. Examples include *first, second, third, next, then, last, later, before, prior to, soon, during, while, after, finally,* as well as specific dates and times.

---

Comprehension Skill

### Compare & Contrast

Authors discuss people, places, objects, or ideas by describing how they are alike and ways they differ.

- To **compare** means to tell how two or more things are alike.

- To **contrast** means to tell how two or more things are different.

- **Signal words** guide you to compare and contrast.

Examples for comparing: *both, like, alike, also, too, share, in the same way,* and *similarly.*

Examples for contrasting: *but, only, unlike, instead, however, in contrast, different, although, on the other hand, as opposed to, neither, whereas, while,* and *rather.*

*Informational Passages for Text Marking & Close Reading: Grade 5*
© 2015 by Scholastic Teaching Resources

# Connections to the Standards

The lessons in this book support the College and Career Readiness Anchor Standards for Reading for students in grades K–12. These broad standards, which serve as the basis of many state standards, were developed to establish rigorous educational expectations with the goal of providing students nationwide with a quality education that prepares them for college and careers. The chart below details how the lessons align with specific reading standards for informational text for students in grade 5.

These materials also address language standards, including skills in the conventions of standard English, knowledge of language, and vocabulary acquisition and use. In addition, students meet writing standards as they answer questions about the passages, demonstrating their ability to convey ideas coherently, clearly, and with support from the text.

| Reading Standards for Informational Text | Passages |
|---|---|
| **Key Ideas and Details** | |
| Quote accurately from a text when explaining what the text says explicitly and when drawing inferences from the text. | 1–20 |
| Determine two or more main ideas of a text and explain how they are supported by key details; summarize the text. | 1–20 |
| Explain the relationships or interactions between two or more individuals, events, ideas, or concepts in a historical, scientific, or technical text based on specific information in the text. | 1–3, 5–18, 20 |
| **Craft and Structure** | |
| Determine the meaning of general academic and domain-specific words and phrases in a text, relevant to a grade 5 topic or subject area. | 1–20 |
| **Integration of Knowledge and Ideas** | |
| Explain how an author uses reasons and evidence to support particular points in a text, identifying which reasons and evidence support which point(s). | 1–20 |
| **Range of Reading and Level of Text Complexity** | |
| By the end of the year, read and comprehend informational texts, including history/social studies, science, and technical texts, at the high end of the grades 4–5 text complexity band independently and proficiently. | 1–20 |

# Main Idea & Details

Every passage has one or more main ideas supported by details. The main idea answers the question, "Who (or What) is this piece about?"

- The **main idea** is the most important point an author makes about a topic. The main idea in most paragraphs is stated in a *topic sentence*. The topic sentence can appear anywhere in a paragraph.

- **Supporting details** are facts, statements, examples, descriptions, and other information that tell more about the main idea.

# Sequence of Events

As you read, notice the order in which things happen or ideas are presented. Think about the *beginning*, *middle*, and *end*.

- **Events** are the important actions that happen.

- The **sequence** is the order in which events happen.

- **Signal words** give clues that help clarify the order of events. Examples include *first, second, third, next, then, last, later, before, prior to, soon, during, while, after, finally*, as well as specific dates and times.

# Fact & Opinion

Do you truly *know* something or do you simply *believe* it? Telling the difference between knowing and believing is a critical reading and thinking skill.

- A **fact** is a statement you can prove or verify. Facts are true and certain.

- An **opinion** is a statement of personal belief or feeling. Opinions vary.

- **Signal words** can help distinguish facts from opinions.

  Examples for facts: *proof, know*, and *discovered*, as well as details, such as dates and ages.

  Examples for opinions: *believe, wish, favor, expect, agree, disagree, probably, seems to, sense, think, viewpoint*, and *feel*.

# Compare & Contrast

Authors discuss people, places, objects, or ideas by describing how they are alike and ways they differ.

- To **compare** means to tell how two or more things are alike.

- To **contrast** means to tell how two or more things are different.

- **Signal words** guide you to compare and contrast.

  Examples for comparing: *both, like, alike, also, too, share, in the same way*, and *similarly*.

  Examples for contrasting: *but, only, unlike, instead, however, in contrast, different, although, on the other hand, as opposed to, neither, whereas, while*, and *rather*.

# Cause & Effect

A text may discuss the relationship between something that happens and any outcomes that follow from it.

- A **cause** is an event, condition, reason, or situation that makes something happen.

- An **effect** is the result of that particular event, condition, reason, or situation.

- **Signal words** are clues that help link a cause with its effects. Examples include *due to, as a result, since, therefore, because of, so, for this reason, consequently, so that, in order to,* and *leads to.*

# Context Clues

Authors may use words you don't know. Search for synonyms, antonyms, explanations, or examples in the nearby text to help you figure out the meaning.

- **Context** refers to the words and sentences around the unfamiliar word.

- **Context clues** are specific indications in the text that can help you unlock the meaning of an unfamiliar word.

# Problem & Solution

This kind of writing presents a challenging situation to engage readers, then offers one or more forms of resolution.

- A **problem** is a difficulty or setback situation that needs fixing.

- A **solution** is a way to deal with the problem to make things better.

- **Signal words** are clues that indicate a problem and its solutions.

   Examples for problems: *question, challenge, dilemma, issue, puzzle, need,* and *trouble.*

   Examples for solutions: *answer, result, one reason, solve, improve, fix, remedy, respond,* and *led to.*

# Summarize

Think about how to retell the key ideas of a passage in your own words. Leave out unimportant details and get to the point.

- The **topic** is the focus of the passage—what it is mainly about.

- **Important details** add more information about the topic.

- A **summary** is a brief statement of the topic using its most essential details. A good summary is short, clear, and recalls what is most important.

*Informational Passages for Text Marking & Close Reading: Grade 5*
© 2015 by Scholastic Teaching Resources

# Make Inferences

Authors may hint at an idea without stating it directly. You must use what you already know about a topic to "read between the lines" to figure out an unstated idea.

- **Text clues** are words or details that help you figure out unstated ideas.

- You **make an inference** by combining text clues with your background knowledge to come to a logical conclusion, or "educated guess."

# Author's Purpose

Every author has goals in mind before writing. Close reading and common sense can help you figure out the author's intention.

- The **author's purpose** is the reason the author chose to write a particular piece. An author may write with more than one purpose.

- The main purposes for writing are to **inform** (tell, describe), to **persuade** (convince, influence), or to **entertain** (amuse, please).

- **Text clues** are words or sentences that reveal the author's purpose.

*Informational Passages for Text Marking & Close Reading: Grade 5*
© 2015 by Scholastic Teaching Resources

# Informational
# Text Passages

Name _____  Date _____

# "The Glory-Beaming Banjo"

**Read the music article.**
**Then follow the directions in the Text Marking box.**

The banjo is a stringed instrument often heard in American folk, bluegrass, and country music. The banjo did not originate in our country, though it is often associated with our music. Rather, musicologists trace the banjo to various locations throughout Africa and the Middle East nearly a thousand years ago.

All early banjos were handmade from local materials. A hollow gourd made a body. An animal skin stretched over the gourd could capture sound and bounce it back. A long stick attached to the gourd served as a neck on which to anchor strings. Three or four strings, made of waxed grass, animal gut, or hair, ran from the body up the neck and were pegged in place. Vibrating strings made the notes.

The banjo probably arrived in America with slaves who had been kidnapped from Africa. Their instruments went by different names, including *bangoe*, *banza*, and *banzil*. Thomas Jefferson's personal writings describe slaves playing "…the Banjar, which they brought hither from Africa."

> The title of this article comes from the writings of humorist Mark Twain.

## Text Marking

Find the main idea and supporting details.

◯ Circle the main idea in each paragraph.

_____ Underline supporting details for each main idea.

People react differently to banjo music. Many enjoy the bright, twangy, jazzy sounds a skilled banjoist can make. Some appreciate how cheerful and clear the banjo sounds. Others find banjo music scratchy, hollow, or tinny. Despite personal preferences, it is fair to regard the banjo as an "outstanding American contribution to the music of folklore."

*Informational Passages for Text Marking & Close Reading: Grade 5*
© 2015 by Scholastic Teaching Resources

Name _____ Date _____

# "The Glory-Beaming Banjo"

▶ **Answer each question. Give evidence from the article.**

**1** Which of the following words is *opposite* in meaning to *anchor,* as it is used in paragraph 2?

○ A. peg          ○ B. secure          ○ C. embark          ○ D. release

What in the text helped you answer? _____

_____

_____

_____

**2** Which statement about the banjo is *not* supported by information in the text?

○ A. Banjo strings vibrate to make its sound.

○ B. It was Mark Twain's favorite instrument.

○ C. American banjos probably had their roots in Africa.

○ D. The banjo is heard in a variety of musical styles.

What in the text helped you answer? _____

_____

_____

_____

**3** In your own words, support the statement about the banjo as an "outstanding American contribution to the music of folklore."

_____

_____

_____

_____

**4** Suggest a different title that would be appropriate for this piece. Explain your thinking.

_____

_____

_____

_____

# Meet a Meat Museum

**Read the museum review.**
**Then follow the directions in the Text Marking box.**

If you like quirky museums, the SPAM® Museum (or Museum of Meat-Themed Awesomeness, as it calls itself) is your kind of place! It's in Austin, Minnesota, the home of Hormel Foods, which manufactures this popular canned meat product. Not surprisingly, Austin calls itself SPAMtown.

Made of pig parts and secret spices, colored and preserved by sodium nitrate, bound by potato starch, and covered in a gelatinous glaze, SPAM® is the monarch of mystery meat. Today, cans of it roll out of Hormel plants at the rate of 44,000 each hour. That's a lot of pre-cooked chopped mystery meat!

The museum is awesome. The first thing to greet you as you enter its lobby is a soaring wall of SPAM® cans. The second is one of the welcoming SPAMbassadors, who will become your guide. After offering slices of SPAM®, he or she will lead you down SPAMburger Alley to see the enormous SPAM® patty hanging from the ceiling. There, too, is a replica SPAM® plant conveyor belt moving hundreds of cans in a perpetual loop.

The museum boasts several other oddly fascinating exhibits. One explains SPAM®'s key role in feeding World War II troops. Another features Slammin' SPAMmy, Hormel's wartime mascot, a glaring cartoon pig. There are also interactive exhibits; one lets visitors try their hand at a mock SPAM® canning assembly line.

And the SPAM® teriyaki at the museum's restaurant is delicious!

> The ® symbol means that the name SPAM is a registered trademark.

## ★ Text Marking ★

Find the main idea and supporting details.

◯  Circle the main idea in each paragraph.

_____  Underline two supporting details for each main idea.

Name _____  Date _____

# Meet a Meat Museum

▶ **Answer each question. Give evidence from the review.**

**1** Which of the following features of the SPAM® Museum make it *quirky* (paragraph 1)?

○ A. It has its own restaurant.        ○ C. Visitors are led by friendly guides.

○ B. It has interactive exhibits.        ○ D. A huge meat patty hangs from the ceiling.

What in the text helped you answer? _____

_____

_____

**2** Who was Slammin' SPAMmy?

○ A. a brave World War II soldier        ○ C. a tour guide in the SPAM® Museum

○ B. a cartoon symbol for SPAM®        ○ D. a baseball player from Austin, Minnesota

What in the text helped you answer? _____

_____

_____

**3** The author of this review has included both facts and opinions. Revisit the text and list three statements of opinion.

_____

_____

_____

_____

**4** This piece is an example of a review of a visit to an actual place. What do you think was the author's reason for writing this review?

_____

_____

_____

_____

*Informational Passages for Text Marking & Close Reading: Grade 5*
© 2015 by Scholastic Teaching Resources

Name _____ Date _____

# Path to the Bigs

**Read the sports article.**
**Then follow the directions in the Text Marking box.**

It's called the "bigs," the "majors," or the "show." By any name, Major League Baseball (MLB) is the dream of talented high school or college ballplayers. For most, it's a long, uphill road to the fame and riches MLB promises. A lucky few make it; most don't.

Long after T-ball, little league, and baseball camp, talented athletes continue to develop their skills in high school and college. For a fortunate few, the dream seems within reach. But the process is highly competitive and involves several stages.

First, a scout from a MLB club learns about promising players and watches them in action. If impressed, the scout informs the team of players with potential. Then, the team drafts the players and signs them to a contract. But it's not for the majors. The prospects next go into the team's minor league system to refine skills.

The levels of Minor League Baseball ascend from Rookie- through Single-, Double-, and Triple-A

Ryan Bradley, pitching for the Richmond Flying Squirrels, a Double-A team of the San Francisco Giants, April 13, 2013

## Text Marking

Find the sequence of events.

☐ Box the signal words.

_____ Underline the important events.

1-2-3 Number the events in the sequence they happen.

leagues. Players generally start at the lowest level and hope to rise. At each level, competition stiffens. Players who improve may advance within the system to get closer to their goal. This can take years, if it happens at all.

Finally, if all the stars align, a player gets "called up" to the majors, where he strives to make the most of this rare opportunity.

*Informational Passages for Text Marking & Close Reading: Grade 5*
© 2015 by Scholastic Teaching Resources

Name _____ Date _____

# Path to the Bigs

▶ **Answer each question. Give evidence from the article.**

**1** What does the author mean by the "uphill road" (paragraph 1) a young baseball player faces on his way to the big leagues?

○ A. Some stops along the way may be at high altitudes.

○ B. The player will have no chance of ever playing for the Dodgers.

○ C. The path to the majors will be hard and demanding.

○ D. The way to the majors gets easier and easier.

What in the text helped you answer? _____

_____

_____

**2** According to the author, which best describes a high school player's chances of reaching the major leagues?

○ A. fifty-fifty          ○ B. slim          ○ C. zero          ○ D. pretty good

What in the text helped you answer? _____

_____

_____

**3** Why does the author use the word *rare* and the expression "if all the stars align" (paragraph 4) when describing a player's opportunity to play for a major league team?

_____

_____

_____

_____

**4** Based on the text, what can you infer about the qualities a person must possess in order to succeed in Major League Baseball?

_____

_____

_____

_____

*Informational Passages for Text Marking & Close Reading: Grade 5*
© 2015 by Scholastic Teaching Resources

# Reimbursement Request

**Read the business e-mail.**

**Then follow the directions in the Text Marking box.**

<table>
<tr><td colspan="2">○ ○ ○</td></tr>
<tr><td>From:</td><td>Susana Ramos&lt;susana_ramos4307@gmail.com&gt;</td></tr>
<tr><td>Sent:</td><td>Tuesday, March 6, 2015</td></tr>
<tr><td>To:</td><td>Kitty Kweezeen&lt;comments@kittykweezeen.com&gt;</td></tr>
</table>

Subject: Request for a refund

---

### Text Marking

Find the sequence of events.

☐    Box the signal words.

_____    <u>Underline</u> the important events.

1-2-3    Number the events in the sequence they happened.

---

Dear Kitty Kweezeen:

For three years, I have been feeding my cat, Stanley, various flavors of your brand of canned food. During that time, he would happily devour whatever I served him and appeared vigorous, bright-eyed, and contented. But yesterday morning, everything changed. I attempted to serve him one of your new flavors: Feline Flambé. Since its principal ingredient is tuna—which Stanley adores—I thought he'd gobble it down. After I filled his bowl, he meowed plaintively, lay down, and later marched away hungry. He never once returned to Feline Flambé that day, which is NOT like Stanley.

So then I discarded all the Feline Flambé, scoured the bowl to remove any bits of food, and served Stanley some of his old standby, your flavor called Kitty Konfetti. But he steadfastly refused that, too.

Finally, I took Stanley to the vet. She confirmed that he is in fine health, so I've begun feeding him a totally different brand of food that he seems to enjoy. Therefore, I respectfully request a return of the $2.28 I spent on the four cans of Feline Flambé, serial number KK0691FF95, that unfortunately went to waste.

Thank you for your attention.

Yours truly,
Susana Ramos

*Informational Passages for Text Marking & Close Reading: Grade 5*
© 2015 by Scholastic Teaching Resources

# Reimbursement Request

▶ **Answer each question. Give evidence from the e-mail.**

**1** Which of the following means the same as *reimbursement*?

○ A. complaint    ○ B. contentment    ○ C. refund    ○ D. request

What in the text helped you answer? _____

_____

_____

_____

**2** Why does the author mention a vet visit with Stanley (paragraph 3)?

○ A. to confirm that Stanley had no health problems

○ B. to prove that Stanley was a well-cared-for pet

○ C. to demand a refund for the cost of the vet visit

○ D. to make the Kitty Kweezeen company feel bad

What in the text helped you answer? _____

_____

_____

**3** Discuss the author's purpose in writing this e-mail.

_____

_____

_____

_____

**4** Evaluate the e-mail Susana wrote. Do you think it effectively makes its case? Explain.

_____

_____

_____

_____

*Informational Passages for Text Marking & Close Reading: Grade 5*
© 2015 by Scholastic Teaching Resources

Name _____ Date _____

# Limit Screen Time?

**Read the health article.**
**Then follow the directions in the Text Marking box.**

In 2011, eight percent of children eight-years old and younger used mobile devices daily. That's according to a report from Common Sense Media. This organization studies issues of concern to teachers and families. By 2013, their report shows that figure had more than doubled. Many pediatricians are concerned. In my view, they are right to be.

These caring doctors contend that this trend is disturbing and needs attention. They focus on data indicating that excessive media use by young children is linked to obesity, lack of sleep, and aggressiveness. They also know that too much media use negatively affects school performance. The American Academy of Pediatrics (AAP) suggests a plan to address the problem.

The doctors urge families to enact rules about TV consumption, texting, Internet surfing, and social media use. They recommend limiting all four. As I see it, they are the people who know best.

These are among the guidelines the AAP proposes:

- No mobile devices should be used during meals and after bedtime.
- Parents should set rules governing TV, cell phone, Internet, and social media use. They should limit that use as well as determine what sites are appropriate for their children.
- There should be no TV or Internet for children younger than two.
- No devices should reside in a young child's bedroom.

I believe that if families follow these rules, children and society will reap the benefits.

> A **pediatrician** is a doctor who specializes in treating children.

## ★ Text Marking ★

Identify the facts and opinions expressed by the author.

| ☐ | Box at least three signal words or phrases. |
| ⬭ | Circle three facts. |
| _____ | <u>Underline</u> three opinions. |

*Informational Passages for Text Marking & Close Reading: Grade 5*
© 2015 by Scholastic Teaching Resources

# Limit Screen Time?

▶ **Answer each question. Give evidence from the article.**

**1** Which of the following might replace *consumption* (paragraph 3) and not change the meaning of the sentence?

   ◯ A. eating     ◯ B. purchasing     ◯ C. viewing     ◯ D. surfing

What in the text helped you answer? _____

_____

_____

**2** Which is *not* a concern of the AAP?

   ◯ A. Excessive media disrupts sleep patterns in young children.

   ◯ B. Excessive media use may make young children act aggressively.

   ◯ C. Excessive media use may cause young children to do poorly in school.

   ◯ D. Excessive media use causes families to spend too much money on media.

What in the text helped you answer? _____

_____

_____

**3** Why do you think the author presented the AAP guidelines in the form of a bulleted list?

_____

_____

_____

**4** Based on your reading of the article, what benefits would you expect children and society to reap if the AAP guidelines were to be followed?

_____

_____

_____

_____

_____

_____

Name _____ Date _____

# Welcome, Leaf-Tailed Gecko!

**Read the science article.**

**Then follow the directions in the Text Marking box.**

What do the Cape Melville leaf-tailed gecko, the raccoon-like olinguito, and Kaweesak's dragon tree have in common? Not much, other than that they are among the thousands of new species scientists discover annually.

Generally, people sense that much of the news about wildlife species is discouraging. Dr. Camilo Mora and other scientists know that, due to habitat loss, as many as 20,000 species go extinct each year. As they see it, new arrivals are a cause for celebration.

The International Institute for Species Exploration works to educate people about biodiversity challenges and what can be done about them. To spark interest, it has come up with a top-ten list of new species. It presented its list to the public on May 23, 2014. Why then, exactly? It was to honor the birthday of the 18th-century

Leaf-tailed gecko from eastern Madagascar

---

**Text Marking**

Identify the facts and opinions in the article.

☐ Box at least three signal words or phrases.

◯ Circle at least three facts.

___ Underline at least three opinions.

---

botanist Carl Linnaeus, whose species-naming system is used to this day. Furthermore, the Institute estimates that as many as 18,000 new species are discovered each year.

Dr. Mora's view is that this may be too high a figure. But to scientists, no matter what the number, more new species are bound to be identified in the future. One of this year's top ten, a tiny bacterium, was found in a sterilized room where NASA works on spacecraft. This discovery—in a sanitized place—makes them assume that new species can pop up just about anywhere!

# Welcome, Leaf-Tailed Gecko!

▶ **Answer each question. Give evidence from the article.**

**1** Which of the following is *not* a synonym for the word *sanitized* (paragraph 4)?

   ◯ A. clean      ◯ B. germ-free      ◯ C. unhealthy      ◯ D. disinfected

What in the text helped you answer? _____

_____

_____

**2** Why did the International Institute for Species Exploration come up with a top-ten list of new species?

   ◯ A. Scientists are fond of making lists.

   ◯ B. They wanted to honor Carl Linnaeus.

   ◯ C. There were only ten new species discovered in 2013.

   ◯ D. They hoped this idea would draw people's attention to biodiversity.

What in the text helped you answer? _____

_____

_____

**3** Paragraph 2 begins like this: "Generally, people sense that much of the news about wildlife species is discouraging." What fact contributes to this attitude?

_____

_____

_____

_____

**4** What fact makes scientists hopeful that they will discover many more species in the future?

_____

_____

_____

_____

_____

*Informational Passages for Text Marking & Close Reading: Grade 5*
© 2015 by Scholastic Teaching Resources

# Symphony or Concerto?

**Read the performance review.**
**Then follow the directions in the Text Marking box.**

Do you know the difference between a symphony and a concerto? An orchestra plays both musical forms, but only one form also requires a soloist. A concert I recently attended demonstrated each form.

The orchestra showcased two compositions played for the first time in the United States. The audience cheered the originality and excitement of each. Both composers, in attendance that evening, received well-earned applause.

The concert began with *Symphony No. 1 in C Minor* by R. Murray Schafer. To me, this rousing piece confirmed his claim that "one makes music to get out of this world." Schafer's work had three movements, each with its own unique feel and color. The entire orchestra played all three movements.

By contrast, Vincent Ho's *The Shaman: Concerto for Percussion and Orchestra* was a lively dialogue between orchestra and soloist. Like the symphony, the concerto had three parts. And as in the symphony,

Percussionist Dame Evelyn Glennie

## Text Marking

Compare and contrast the symphony and concerto as described in this review.

☐ Box at least three signal words or phrases.

◯ Circle two ways they are alike.

_____ Underline one way they are different.

the orchestra played, but the true star was Dame Evelyn Glennie, the gifted Scottish percussionist. Glennie performed extended solos on an army of instruments, including drums, chimes, bells, bowls, and bongos. She moved among them like a dancer—sometimes floating, other times making powerful gestures.

As in any concerto, the orchestra and soloist in *The Shaman* sometimes played together. Glennie's dazzling performance made the piece unforgettable, transporting the audience with pure joy.

# Symphony or Concerto?

▶ **Answer each question. Give evidence from the review.**

**1** Which of the following word can replace *movements* (paragraph 3) without changing the meaning of the sentence?

  ○ A. plays      ○ B. parts      ○ C. activities      ○ D. dialogues

What in the text helped you answer? _____

_____

_____

**2** For what audience do you think the author wrote this review?

  ○ A. Dame Evelyn Glennie      ○ C. people who enjoy going to concerts

  ○ B. music scholars      ○ D. people who know nothing about orchestra music

What in the text helped you answer? _____

_____

_____

**3** Describe the author's opinion of the concert that evening.

_____

_____

_____

_____

**4** Look back at your text markings and think about the ideas in the review. In your own words, summarize the similarities and the major difference between the symphony and the concerto the author reviewed.

_____

_____

_____

_____

_____

_____

_____

Name _____ Date _____

# Before Smart Phones

**Read the technology essay.**
**Then follow the directions in the Text Marking box.**

This rotary dial phone was introduced in 1949.

Telephones had already made the world smaller when your grandparents chatted on them. People used phones to talk to friends on the next block, in the next town, even in another country. Like today's smart phones, Grandma's phone provided convenient communication at any time.

When she was a girl, Grandma probably used a rotary phone. Connected by wires to central switching stations, this kind of phone had a heavy base that sat on a table. Its handset, bulky and as long as a hero sandwich, held both the receiver for listening and the transmitter for speaking. Yet there was nothing to press to make a call. Rather, Grandma dialed each digit of a phone number by poking her finger into a numbered hole, turning the dial clockwise to the finger stop, and letting go. After all digits were dialed, the call went through.

Many homes had just one rotary phone that a family shared. Compact, but heavy with moving parts inside, the phone stayed put. You didn't take it with you; you used the phone wherever it had been installed.

Those dinosaurs are barely recognizable today. Compared with them, digital smart phones are sleek, lightweight, multipurpose, and portable. One-piece smart phones have touchscreens rather than round dials. Unlike rotary phones, wireless smart phones can take messages, send e-mails, access the Internet, play music, snap photos, and hold games. And yes, they make and receive calls, too.

---

## Text Marking

Compare and contrast the phones people used two generations ago with digital smart phones.

☐ Box at least four signal words or phrases.

◯ Circle two ways they are alike.

_____ Underline three ways they are different.

Name _____ Date _____

# Before Smart Phones

▶ **Answer each question. Give evidence from the essay.**

**1** Which of the following words best helps you determine the meaning of the word *rotary* (paragraph 2)?

⬡ A. notate      ⬡ B. rotation      ⬡ C. rotten      ⬡ D. rotund

What in the text helped you answer? _____

_____

_____

**2** Which is a way in which rotary phones and smart phones are alike?

⬡ A. Both are wireless.

⬡ B. Both can be used to receive and leave messages.

⬡ C. Both provide a means of convenient communication.

⬡ D. Both must be used only where they have been installed.

What in the text helped you answer? _____

_____

_____

**3** The author begins the essay by saying that "telephones had already made the world smaller...." What does this expression really mean?

_____

_____

_____

_____

**4** In your own words, summarize the key contrasts between rotary phones and smart phones.

_____

_____

_____

_____

_____

_____

# Space and the Human Body

**Read the newspaper article.**
**Then follow the directions in the Text Marking box.**

Humans are not made for space travel. The microgravity environment of outer space causes several challenging health hazards.

One problem is swelled heads. Reduced gravity affects the water that makes up nearly two-thirds of our bodies. In space, fluids, including blood, rise up into the skull, puffing it up. Correspondingly, the legs begin to deteriorate as they lose their normal amount of fluid. Bones lose density and weaken. "It kind of feels like you would feel if you hung upside down for a couple of minutes," one astronaut explained.

In addition, there can be vision issues. It seems that some astronauts' eyeballs flatten and, as a result, they become farsighted—they can't easily see things close-up. But the most serious issue is radiation. For without the protection of our atmosphere, space travelers are exposed to harmful doses that increase their chances of getting cancer.

NASA scientists are working hard to solve the problems they are aware of. But there are always the unforeseen ones, those they call the "unknown unknowns." One unknown, for instance, is how additional time astronauts spend in space will affect the problems described above.

Time for solutions is short, for NASA's plan is to send astronauts to Mars within 20 years or so. Thus far, the longest anyone has spent in space is about 438 days. The journey to Mars would take 2.5 years.

### Blood Flow in the Body

Effects of gravity on Earth

Effects of microgravity in space

### Text Marking

Find a cause-and-effect relationship.

☐ Box at least four signal words or phrases.

◯ Circle the cause.

_____ Underline at least four effects.

# Space and the Human Body

▶ **Answer each question. Give evidence from the article.**

**1**   A person who is farsighted _____.

    ○ A. must have spent time in outer space

    ○ B. has trouble reading small print on a label

    ○ C. cannot see clearly across a street

    ○ D. feels like he or she is hanging upside down

    What in the text helped you answer? _____

    _____

**2**   Which of the following is *not* an effect of space travel on the human body?

    ○ A. swollen feet       ○ C. flattened eyeballs

    ○ B. weakened bones     ○ D. exposure to excess radiation

    What in the text helped you answer? _____

    _____

**3**   Describe how the illustration clarifies one of the problems caused by microgravity during space travel.

    _____

    _____

    _____

    _____

    _____

**4**   Why did the author end the article by telling how long it would take to journey to Mars?

    _____

    _____

    _____

    _____

*Informational Passages for Text Marking & Close Reading: Grade 5*
© 2015 by Scholastic Teaching Resources

Name _____  Date _____

# Pocket Change

**Read the culture article.**
**Then follow the directions in the Text Marking box.**

Since the emergence of e-books and e-readers, more people than ever are reading. But this recent development was not the first sea change in Americans' reading habits. One significant shift took place in 1938, when paperback books first made their appearance.

Before Robert Fair de Graff, backed by a large publishing company, launched Pocket Books, it was challenging for most people to obtain their own books. For one thing, there were only about 500 bookstores in the entire country. For another, hardcover books were expensive.

The new paperbacks, on the other hand, were much cheaper and, at a size of 4 inches by 6 inches, much smaller, lighter, and easier to carry around. They were now being sold not only in bookstores, but also in supermarkets, department stores, even drug stores. For these reasons, reading habits changed. People who'd never read much before now began expanding their personal libraries. Sales of paperbacks surged. In fact, the demand for these less bulky books often exceeded the supply.

---

**Text Marking**

Find the cause-and-effect relationships.

☐   Box the signal words.

◯   Circle the cause in each paragraph.

____   <u>Underline</u> the effects.

---

However, the success of paperbacks eventually leveled off. Due to the profits they foresaw, large media companies rushed in to buy up smaller paperback book companies. This led to a steady rise in paperback prices. Soon, paperbacks began to approach the hardcovers in price. Although paperbacks are still commonplace, they are no longer cheap.

But these days people have their e-books and e-readers.

*Informational Passages for Text Marking & Close Reading: Grade 5*
© 2015 by Scholastic Teaching Resources

# Pocket Change

▶ **Answer each question. Give evidence from the article.**

**1** What is *true* about reading today?

⃝ A. More people read paperbacks today than any other kind of books.

⃝ B. With competition from e-books, paperback prices have dropped.

⃝ C. There are more readers now than there ever have been.

⃝ D. Readers are finding paperbacks harder to find.

What in the text helped you answer? _____

_____

_____

**2** What is *not* true about Americans' reading habits prior to the arrival of paperback books?

⃝ A. Many people had a difficult time even finding books to buy.

⃝ B. Most people didn't know how to read.

⃝ C. Many people couldn't afford the hardcover books.

⃝ D. People purchased fewer books than they did after paperbacks appeared.

What in the text helped you answer? _____

_____

_____

**3** What do you suppose the author means by a "sea change" (paragraph 1) in reading habits?

_____

_____

_____

**4** What explains the effect that paperbacks and then e-readers have had on Americans' reading habits?

_____

_____

_____

_____

Name _____ Date _____

# Bigger Than Big

**Read the word origin article.**
**Then follow the directions in the Text Marking box.**

As any cook or farmer can confirm, "jumbo" eggs are much bigger than large eggs. The biggest jets in a fleet are nicknamed "jumbo" jets. Most people use the word *jumbo* to describe anything bigger than usual. But how did this now-common adjective get its start?

Some English speakers link the term *jumbo* to a famous African pachyderm by that name. That elephant lives on to this day, thanks to the fame it earned as part of P.T. Barnum's "Greatest Show on Earth." The original Jumbo was captured by an African hunting party in 1861. At the time, this 13,000-pound behemoth was one of the largest elephants ever seen in that part of the world. The locals called him Jumbo—an English spelling of the Swahili word for chief.

Jumbo was sent to a zoo in Paris, and later transferred to a London zoo. But he was a cantankerous captive. The keeper worried that Jumbo's grouchy and unpredictable behavior might make him too dangerous for a zoo. So the grand tusker was sold to P.T. Barnum, who featured him to amaze circus audiences.

Or so the origin story goes…

Another conjecture about the roots of *jumbo* traces the word to a London zookeeper. This notion states that *jumbo* was based on the Zulu word *jumba*, which means a large parcel. No matter the theory, there's no question that Jumbo certainly was enormous!

Jumbo the elephant in the 1880s

## Text Marking

Use context clues to unlock word meanings.

◯ Circle the words *cantankerous* and *conjecture*.

_____ Underline context clues for each word.

*Informational Passages for Text Marking & Close Reading: Grade 5*
© 2015 by Scholastic Teaching Resources

Name _____  Date _____

# Bigger Than Big

▶ **Answer each question. Give evidence from the article.**

**1** According to the article, what was the main reason Jumbo was sold to P.T. Barnum?

○ A. At 13,000 pounds, Jumbo was too big for a zoo.

○ B. Not enough people in London visited Jumbo at the zoo.

○ C. The zoo was afraid to keep the unpredictable elephant.

○ D. P.T. Barnum needed an elephant for his "Greatest Show on Earth."

What in the text helped you answer? _____

_____

_____

**2** Which pair of words shows two synonyms?

○ A. *unpredictable* and *behemoth*          ○ C. *cantankerous* and *behavior*

○ B. *parcel* and *enormous*          ○ D. *conjecture* and *notion*

What in the text helped you answer? _____

_____

_____

**3** Explain how you determined the meaning of *pachyderm* (paragraph 2).

_____

_____

_____

_____

**4** Why do you think the author of this article began with familiar examples of the word *jumbo* in our language today?

_____

_____

_____

# The Shadow Catcher

**Read the sociology essay.**
**Then follow the directions in the Text Marking box.**

His goal was to live among Native Americans and document their traditional ways of life. That was a formidable and perilous undertaking in 1900. But when Seattle-based photographer Edward Curtis finally completed this epic project, it was hailed by the *New York Herald* as "…the most ambitious enterprise in publishing since…the King James Bible."

Curtis essentially left behind a successful photography business to pursue his dream. With support from President Theodore Roosevelt and funds from the wealthy J. P. Morgan, he eagerly began his quest. He packed his photography and recording equipment, gathered supplies, assistants, and interpreters, and ventured into Indian territories. Rugged terrain, illness, intense heat, freezing temperatures, and suspicious native groups did not deter him. Determined to capture lifestyles that he knew would soon vanish, Curtis persevered. The results were astonishing.

Curtis took this photo of family members from the Piegan tribe in 1910.

## Text Marking

Use context clues to unlock word meanings.

◯   Circle the words *perilous* and *capture*.

_____   Underline context clues for each word.

From the Inuit of the far north to the Havasupai within the depths of the Grand Canyon, Curtis visited more than 80 tribes. Over 30 years, he took 40,000 photos and collected 10,000 audio recordings of music and language. Notable leaders like Geronimo, Red Cloud, and Chief Joseph posed for him. He got on well with his subjects. They called him the Shadow Catcher.

Curtis's finished work amounted to 20 volumes of pictures and text. His remarkable achievement is the most definitive archive of American Indian life. It remains a priceless cultural treasure.

*Informational Passages for Text Marking & Close Reading: Grade 5*
© 2015 by Scholastic Teaching Resources

Name _____ Date _____

# The Shadow Catcher

▶ **Answer each question. Give evidence from the essay.**

**1** Which word could replace *perilous* in paragraph 1?

   ○ A. expensive    ○ B. hazardous    ○ C. lengthy    ○ D. unusual

What in the text helped you answer? _____

_____

_____

**2** What is the meaning of the word *capture* as it is used in paragraph 2?

   ○ A. catch    ○ B. seize    ○ C. acquire    ○ D. document

What in the text helped you answer? _____

_____

_____

_____

**3** What are some remarkable things about Curtis's quest and his achievements?

_____

_____

_____

_____

_____

_____

**4** Use context clues in the essay to explain the meaning of *persevered* (paragraph 2) in your own words.

_____

_____

_____

_____

_____

_____

Name _____ Date _____

# A Worldwide Pickle

**Read the nutrition article.**
**Then follow the directions in the Text Marking box.**

Nature demands that living things must eat to survive. This might seem easy in a modern world of freezers, supermarkets, and restaurants. But in the past, the problem was that much food spoiled before anyone could eat it. Our ancestors knew that without food, they would die. So they needed to find ways to treat foods to make them last. They had to preserve enough food in good times to survive harsh winters, droughts, natural disasters, and seasonal shortages.

One early answer to making food last was *pickling*. Pickling is a way to preserve foods by curing them in vinegar and/or salt to prevent spoiling. Vinegar is an acid that kills most bacteria. Salt dries food out and aids in the growth of "good" bacteria that protect against the "bad" bacteria that cause rot. Nearly every culture in the world developed pickled foods.

Science has since proven that pickling not only makes food last longer, it also makes some of it easier to digest. In fact, certain foods become more nutritious after they have been pickled. Pickling can also convert inedible foods, such as some roots or plants, into healthy new forms.

cabbage  onions  kimchi

chutney  corn  pickles

Which of these pickled foods have you tried?

## Text Marking

Find the problem and solution.

☐ Box the signal words.

◯ Circle the problem.

___ Underline the solution.

### Pickled Foods From Around the World

| Name | Made From... | Common in... |
| --- | --- | --- |
| *chutney* | fruits/vegetables | India |
| *itlog na maalat* | eggs | The Philippines |
| *jerky* | meat/fish | The Americas |
| *kimchi* | cabbage/radish | Korea |
| *sill* | herring | Sweden |
| *umeboshi* | plums | Japan |

*Informational Passages for Text Marking & Close Reading: Grade 5*
© 2015 by Scholastic Teaching Resources

Name _____  Date _____

# A Worldwide Pickle

▶ **Answer each question. Give evidence from the article.**

**1** Something that is *inedible* (paragraph 3) cannot be _____.

○ A. eaten      ○ B. grown      ○ C. frozen      ○ D. preserved

What in the text helped you answer? _____

_____

_____

_____

**2** Which of the following foods could appear in the chart?

○ A. orange juice      ○ B. corn muffin      ○ C. ice cream      ○ D. salt pork

What in the text helped you answer? _____

_____

_____

_____

**3** Why do you think the author includes the chart of pickled foods?

_____

_____

_____

_____

_____

**4** The title of this article has a double meaning. Explain the two meanings.

_____

_____

_____

_____

_____

_____

_____

*Informational Passages for Text Marking & Close Reading: Grade 5*
© 2015 by Scholastic Teaching Resources

Name _____   Date _____

# Space Junk

**Read the environment essay.**
**Then follow the directions in the Text Marking box.**

All countries that send objects into space confront a serious problem: space junk. The "junk" consists of parts of rockets, debris from launches, dead satellites, and other manufactured items afloat in space. There may well be half a million pieces of dangerous waste in orbit. As you might expect, countries around the world are concerned. Many are working on solutions to destroy the detritus.

Japan's space agency has built an electromagnetic tether. This giant steel and aluminum net, nearly half a mile wide, would orbit in space and attract metallic fragments as it travels. Once full of waste, the net would fall back into the Earth's atmosphere. The gathered fragments would burn upon re-entry. If this net idea works, Japan intends to build a much larger one.

A Swiss company proposes a different answer. It is developing a spacecraft that would act as a huge catcher's mitt to snatch harmful debris. Like the Japanese net, the Swiss "glove" would fall back into Earth's atmosphere, destroying its contents in the process.

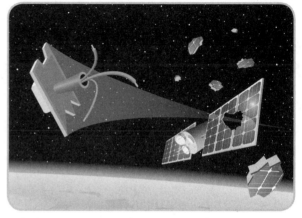

Illustration of space debris destroying part of a satellite

---

### ★ Text Marking ★

Find the problem and solutions.

[  ]  Box the signal words.

( ◯ )  Circle the problem.

_____  Underline the solutions.

---

Not surprisingly, scientists in the United States are also seeking solutions to the challenge of hazardous space rubble. One team's curious proposal may provide the most captivating resolution— and would save on fuel, too. Its plan is to build what it calls the Space Sweeper with Sling-Sat. Acting like a gigantic sling-shot, this gizmo would capture objects and fling them toward the Earth's atmosphere.

*Informational Passages for Text Marking & Close Reading: Grade 5*

Name _____    Date _____

# Space Junk

▶ **Answer each question. Give evidence from the essay.**

**1** Which context clue helps you determine the meaning of *detritus* (paragraph 1)?

○ A. electromagnetic tether ○ C. companies are concerned

○ B. dangerous waste in orbit ○ D. confront a serious problem

What in the text helped you answer? _____

_____

_____

**2** Which is the most significant way that the solution of U.S. scientists differs from the others described in the essay?

○ A. It costs far more than the other two.

○ B. The other inventions are not yet named.

○ C. It is closer to being ready to send into space.

○ D. It would fling junk back toward Earth instead of trapping it.

What in the text helped you answer? _____

_____

_____

**3** In what ways are the Japanese and Swiss ideas similar?

_____

_____

_____

_____

**4** Make an inference. Why do you think nations are working so hard to develop ways to rid space of its junk?

_____

_____

_____

_____

_____

*Informational Passages for Text Marking & Close Reading: Grade 5*
© 2015 by Scholastic Teaching Resources

Name _____ Date _____

# "Creative Elegance"

**Read the fine arts essay.**
**Then follow the directions in the Text Marking box.**

"My journey begins with the line," states Salma Arastu. In her art, Arastu uses looping, continuous lines to suggest her hope for a world united in peace. Professor Richard Viera of Lehigh University wrote that her art "...reflects, as well as transcends, all barriers with compassion and creative elegance." I resolved to learn more about this California-based Hindu-Muslim painter, sculptor, and poet.

Artist Salma Arastu at work on a painting

### Text Marking

Summarize the text.

◯ Circle the topic.

_____ Underline important details.

Born in India in 1950, Salma Arastu was the tenth and youngest child in her family. Due to a birth defect, she had no fingers on her left hand. Her mother helped her view this challenge as a blessing, and encouraged Salma to seek her purpose in life. Salma began drawing loops and curves and never stopped. Art helped her explore, accept, and embrace the world in all its variations. She says that her art attempts to "build bridges between all faiths and form a dialogue of understanding."

I visited The Triton Museum of Art in Santa Clara to see her one-woman show. There, I also learned that she does digital art and has written and illustrated greeting cards and books of poetry.

Arastu's graceful paintings moved me deeply. I believe that she is one of the finest artists working today. Her canvases are both alive and soothingly peaceful. In some, she paints lacy Arabic calligraphy atop softly colored backgrounds. Even without knowing the meanings of the words, the sheer beauty inspired me.

# "Creative Elegance"

▶ **Answer each question. Give evidence from the essay.**

**1** What do you think the phrase "transcends all barriers" in paragraph 1 means?

○ A. to accept challenges      ○ C. to rise above obstacles

○ B. to learn many languages   ○ D. to ignore the world's problems

What in the text helped you answer? _____

_____

**2** In which way was Salma Arastu's mother an inspiration to her?

○ A. She didn't let her own birth defect stop her.

○ B. She told Salma to focus her art toward peace.

○ C. She was a talented and experienced artist herself.

○ D. She lovingly encouraged her daughter to seek her path in life.

What in the text helped you answer? _____

_____

_____

**3** Look back at your text markings. Write a one-paragraph summary of the key information provided in the essay.

_____

_____

_____

_____

_____

_____

**4** The essay includes some opinions the author expresses. Identify one of these opinions, and explain how you know it is *not* a fact.

_____

_____

_____

_____

*Informational Passages for Text Marking & Close Reading: Grade 5*
© 2015 by Scholastic Teaching Resources

Name _____ Date _____

# Animal Weather Forecasters?

**Read the magazine article.**
**Then follow the directions in the Text Marking box.**

Will earthworms wriggle out of the ground prior to a flood? Will sharks swim to deeper waters before a hurricane? Do animals actually have powers beyond those that guide them in their daily lives, powers that enable them to predict natural disasters like earthquakes or hurricanes? The short answer is probably "No." But the long answer is more complex.

Scientists are skeptical that animals have a special sense that enables them to predict the weather. But they know that many animals have more highly developed senses than humans do, and are capable of detecting signals of impending weather change sooner than we can. Some, like dogs, pick up infrasonic sound waves—sounds that are at lower frequencies than we can hear. Others, like the frogs that go silent before a storm, can detect differences in air pressure. However they get their signals, animals learn to associate them with danger. Those signals alert them that it is time to move to a safer area.

All animals have a strong survival instinct, but can they predict weather patterns? Does a groundhog know what kind of spring lies ahead? Will a black bear choose its winter den depending on how cold the upcoming winter promises to be? Not likely, say the scientists. But if you spot a cluster of birds hunkering down outside your window, you'd be wise to take your umbrella.

Changes in air pressure may cause seagulls to seek shelter on land.

## Text Marking

Summarize the text.

⬭ Circle the topic.

_____ Underline important details.

*Informational Passages for Text Marking & Close Reading: Grade 5*
© 2015 by Scholastic Teaching Resources

Name _____ Date _____

# Animal Weather Forecasters?

▶ **Answer each question. Give evidence from the article.**

**1** Which is the best synonym for the word *impending* in paragraph 2?

○ A. major ○ B. distant ○ C. natural ○ D. coming

What in the text helped you answer? _____

_____

_____

**2** Which statement is *not* supported by information in the text?

○ A. Changes in air pressure may help some animals detect signals of weather change.

○ B. Animals can probably predict weather patterns.

○ C. Many animals have sharper senses than humans do.

○ D. Some frogs stop croaking when they sense a storm is coming.

What in the text helped you answer? _____

_____

_____

**3** Look back at your text markings. Write a one-paragraph summary of the key information provided in the article.

_____

_____

_____

_____

_____

**4** Why does the author use words like *probably*, *skeptical*, and *not likely* when discussing views on animal behaviors involving weather change?

_____

_____

_____

# ¡Si, Se Pueda!

**Read the biographical sketch.**
**Then follow the directions in the Text Marking box.**

"We draw our strength from the very despair in which we have been forced to live," said activist Cesar Chavez. And he knew what he was talking about.

Chavez was born in Arizona in 1927 to immigrant parents. They owned a small farm and lived in an adobe house built by his grandfather. Soon, hard times forced his family to relocate to California, where they moved from farm to farm picking crops. Chavez understood firsthand the tough lives migrant workers led. Hardened by his experiences, he dedicated himself to improving those wretched conditions.

Cesar Chavez speaking to migrant workers in 1985

Migrant workers had it rough. Their camps were unsanitary. Their labor was long and backbreaking and the pay meager. In addition, the migrants faced bitter prejudice. Chavez began his work for change.

Drawing on what he observed in the civil rights movement, he organized the powerless workers to fight the powerful growers nonviolently. Chavez organized protest marches, boycotts, and hunger strikes. Through his dogged efforts—including a lengthy hunger strike of his own—and against great odds, Chavez accomplished

---

### Text Marking

Make an inference: What is an activist?

_____ Underline text clues.

 Think about what you already know.

---

many of his goals. He died in 1993, a hero who left America a better place than he found it.

During his courageous efforts to win improvements for migrant workers, Cesar Chavez coined the phrase *¡Si, se pueda!* which means "Yes, it can be done!" This inspiring slogan still rings true today.

*Informational Passages for Text Marking & Close Reading: Grade 5*
© 2015 by Scholastic Teaching Resources

Name _____  Date _____

# ¡Si, Se Pueda!

▶ **Answer each question. Give evidence from the biographical sketch.**

**1** Which of the following statements would Cesar Chavez agree with?

○ A. The poor cannot better their lives.

○ B. Adversity can be a source of inspiration.

○ C. The strategy of nonviolence is not effective.

○ D. The powerless are forever held back by the powerful.

What in the text helped you answer? _____

_____

_____

**2** Which of these words is the best synonym for *dogged* (paragraph 4)?

○ A. backbreaking      ○ B. half-hearted      ○ C. persistent      ○ D. loyal

What in the text helped you answer? _____

_____

_____

**3** Look back at your text markings and consider your own knowledge. What is an activist?

_____

_____

_____

_____

**4** Based on the information in this biographical sketch, describe what it means to be a migrant worker.

_____

_____

_____

_____

_____

*Informational Passages for Text Marking & Close Reading: Grade 5*
© 2015 by Scholastic Teaching Resources

# Malala Day

**Read the blog post.**
**Then follow the directions in the Text Marking box.**

On July 12, 2013, the United Nations honored an innocent Pakistani teen whose near-death focused worldwide attention on the need for education. "Malala Day" was held to pay tribute to Malala Yousafzai. When she was fifteen, extremists opposing education for girls attempted to kill her. Though gravely wounded, Malala recovered to become a courageous champion for the rights of millions of girls worldwide whose gender denies them a chance at an education.

Malala Yousafzai speaking at the United Nations

In 2014, Malala was awarded the Nobel Peace Prize, the youngest person ever to win this honor.

It was Malala's sixteenth birthday that day, and my eleventh. She quietly and modestly addressed hundreds of people in her first public speech since the cruel attack on her the October before. She never voiced anger, nor did she call for revenge. She spoke passionately about her goals for education, equality, and peace. One sentence she uttered that day became a slogan: *One child, one teacher, one pen, and one book can change the world.*

Malala Yousafzai gently but firmly denounced terrorism and urged greater respect and dignity for all people. Listening to her speech online gave me goosebumps and brought tears to my eyes. She seemed so mature and peaceful, yet she's the same age as my sister. It made me realize how powerful one girl, a deeply-held belief, and thoughtful words can be. She is a model to me of bravery, self-esteem, and hope.

## Text Marking

Make an inference: What sort of person is Malala Yousafzai?

_____ Underline text clues.

 Think about what you already know.

*Informational Passages for Text Marking & Close Reading: Grade 5*
© 2015 by Scholastic Teaching Resources

# Malala Day

▶ **Answer each question. Give evidence from the blog.**

**1** Which of the following would make a suitable alternate title for this piece?

○ A. Malala's Amazing Recovery     ○ C. How Malala Spent her Birthday

○ B. Malala Rages Against Violence     ○ D. Malala Calls for Equality in Education

What in the text helped you answer? _____

_____

_____

**2** According to its use in this blog, which has the same meaning as *slogan* (paragraph 2)?

○ A. motto     ○ B. poem     ○ C. prayer     ○ D. advertisement

What in the text helped you answer? _____

_____

_____

**3** Based on what you understand about Malala, infer why she did not call for revenge.

_____

_____

_____

_____

_____

**4** Based on the text, what inference can you make about the character of Malala Yousafzai?

_____

_____

_____

_____

_____

_____

_____

*Informational Passages for Text Marking & Close Reading: Grade 5*
© 2015 by Scholastic Teaching Resources

# Food Without a Face

**Read the business letter.**
**Then follow the directions in the Text Marking box.**

To Principal Fergerson:

    I respectfully request that you and our cafeteria staff rethink the lunch program. My Buddhist family follows a vegetarian diet. We believe that animals are living beings that we should not kill and eat for food. My dad says, "Don't eat anything with a face." This may sound strange to you. However, it helps us remember to avoid eating beef, lamb, pork, goat, chicken, turkey, and fish.

    Our daily school lunches almost always offer some kind of meat, such as hot dogs, burgers, chicken, or fish sticks. I cannot eat any of these foods without violating my beliefs. I do not expect all meals to be vegetarian, since I realize that not all students believe as I do. But I'd find it much easier if the menu included meatless choices.

    Do consider adding simple options for me and my brother Kai, and others I know who wish or need to forgo meat. Please provide sliced cheeses or peanut butter for sandwiches, hard-boiled eggs, yogurt, hummus, or veggie wraps. Why not serve fresh salad with meatless add-ons, like nuts, cheese, avocado, lentils, bean sprouts, or tofu? That would surely appeal to many students and teachers, including those who do eat meat.

    Thanks for considering my request. My parents say they'll happily offer some easy, kid-friendly ideas.

Yours truly,

Charini Anzan

Mr. Delgado's Grade 5 class

Veggie wraps

## Text Marking

Check to identify the author's <u>two</u> purposes.

☐    to entertain (E)

☐    to inform (I)

☐    to persuade (P)

_____ <u>Underline</u> text clues for this purpose. Write E, I, or P in the margin beside each clue.

Name _____     Date _____

# Food Without a Face

▶ **Answer each question. Give evidence from the letter.**

**1** Which of the following would be *violating* (paragraph 2) Charini Anzan's beliefs?

○ A. eating a cheeseburger                ○ C. reading a book about chicken farms

○ B. buying a chocolate candy bar      ○ D. ordering a grilled-cheese sandwich

What in the text helped you answer? _____

_____

_____

**2** According to her letter, Charini follows a vegetarian diet because it is _____.

○ A. better for our planet          ○ C. less costly than eating meat

○ B. a healthier way to eat        ○ D. in keeping with her family's beliefs

What in the text helped you answer? _____

_____

_____

**3** What inference can you make about the author based on the points she made in her letter? Explain.

_____

_____

_____

_____

**4** Write a brief summary of the main point of Charini's request to Principal Fergerson.

_____

_____

_____

_____

_____

*Informational Passages for Text Marking & Close Reading: Grade 5*
© 2015 by Scholastic Teaching Resources

Name _____ Date _____

# He Did All That?

**Read the history essay.**
**Then follow the directions in the Text Marking box.**

Diplomat, philosopher, and businessman, Benjamin Franklin was the foremost American of his day. He was a pivotal figure in colonial and revolutionary times, and the architect of an alliance with France that ensured the colonies' independence from England. A much-admired figure in politics, this legendary American was a scientific and engineering genius, too.

The list and breadth of his inventions are astonishing. Let's start with electricity, which Franklin did not invent. But he did grasp its properties, coining several terms, such as *battery*, *charge*, and *conductor*, in the process. He applied his understanding to invent the lightning rod, a metal device that protected houses from the "mischief" of lightning.

Franklin could not see clearly up close. When he invented bifocals—glasses with distinct upper and lower halves, one for distance, one for reading—he had his own condition in mind. To advance his love for swimming, he built fins that attached to the hands. And when he noticed, after eight transatlantic crossings, that speed was affected by the Gulf Stream, he mapped that critical coastal current.

Then there was the Franklin stove. This iron structure provided better airflow and longer-lasting heat than a fireplace did. He also designed the glass armonica, a musical instrument made of glass bowls color-coded by note. And he built an odometer to record the distance carriage wheels traveled.

Where did he get the time?

Benjamin Franklin playing his glass armonica

## Text Marking

Check to identify the author's purpose.

☐ to entertain (E)

☐ to inform (I)

☐ to persuade (P)

_____ Underline text clues for each purpose. Write E, I, or P in the margin beside each clue.

*Informational Passages for Text Marking & Close Reading: Grade 5*
© 2015 by Scholastic Teaching Resources

Name _____     Date _____

# He Did All That?

▶ **Answer each question. Give evidence from the essay.**

**1** Someone who is described as *pivotal* (paragraph 1) is _____.

◯ A. flexible and strong      ◯ C. political or philosophical

◯ B. central or essential      ◯ D. nearsighted or farsighted

What in the text helped you answer? _____

_____

_____

**2** Which is the most likely purpose for the last sentence of the essay?

◯ A. to encourage readers to response to the essay

◯ B. to urge readers to learn more about Benjamin Franklin

◯ C. to suggest that Franklin may have invented a type of clock or watch

◯ D. to emphasize the remarkable number of Franklin's accomplishments

What in the text helped you answer? _____

_____

_____

**3** Why does the author put the word *mischief* (paragraph 2) within quotations marks?

_____

_____

_____

**4** Look back at your markings regarding author's purpose. Summarize the author's purpose for writing this essay.

_____

_____

_____

_____

_____

_____

*Informational Passages for Text Marking & Close Reading: Grade 5*
© 2015 by Scholastic Teaching Resources

# Answer Key

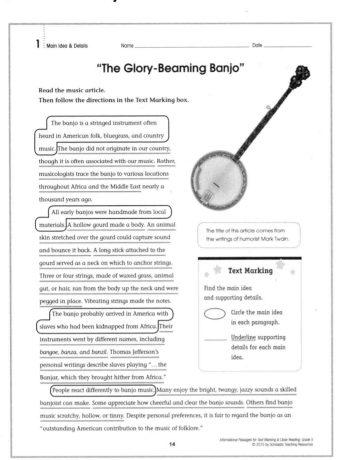

## Passage 1: "The Glory-Beaming Banjo"

**1**. D; Sample answer: Something that is anchored is held in place or secured. And I can see from the photo that the neck holds the strings in place. *Release* is the opposite of *anchor*.

**2**. B; Sample answer: There is no information about Mark Twain's musical preferences in this piece, though the title uses his words.

**3**. Sample answer: Banjos were handcrafted by people so they could make their own music. Banjos were used in many different kinds of traditional music and widely appreciated.

**4**. Sample answer: I might call it "All About the Banjo" because that's what this article does—it gives background, explains how the banjo is made and played, and discusses a variety of reactions to banjo music.

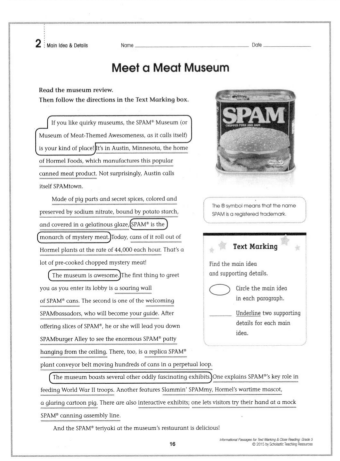

◀ Sample Text Markings

## Passage 2: Meet a Meat Museum

**1**. D; Sample answer: The other choices describe features typical of most museums.

**2**. B; Sample answer: In paragraph 4, the author describes Slammin' SPAMmy as "Hormel's wartime mascot, a glaring cartoon pig."

**3**. Sample answer: Here are three opinions I found: In paragraph 2, the author calls SPAM® the "monarch of mystery meat." In paragraph 3, the author calls the museum "awesome." In the last line, the author says that SPAM® teriyaki is delicious.

**4**. Sample answer: I think the author wanted to give information about an interesting and unusual place people might not know about. The review makes the place sound fun to visit, goofy, educational, and entertaining.

*Informational Passages for Text Marking & Close Reading: Grade 5*
© 2015 by Scholastic Teaching Resources

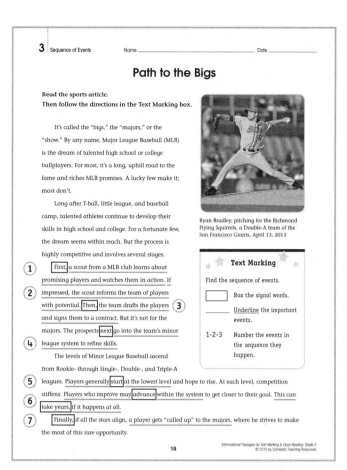

**3** Sequence of Events · Name _____ Date _____

## Path to the Bigs

**Read the sports article.
Then follow the directions in the Text Marking box.**

It's called the "bigs," the "majors," or the "show." By any name, Major League Baseball (MLB) is the dream of talented high school or college ballplayers. For most, it's a long, uphill road to the fame and riches MLB promises. A lucky few make it; most don't.

Long after T-ball, little league, and baseball camp, talented athletes continue to develop their skills in high school and college. For a fortunate few, the dream seems within reach. But the process is highly competitive and involves several stages.

(1) First, a scout from a MLB club learns about promising players and watches them in action. If (2) impressed, the scout informs the team of players with potential. Then, the team drafts the players (3) and signs them to a contract. But it's not for the majors. The prospects next go into the team's minor (4) league system to refine skills.

The levels of Minor League Baseball ascend from Rookie- through Single-, Double-, and Triple-A (5) leagues. Players generally start at the lowest level and hope to rise. At each level, competition (6) stiffens. Players who improve may advance within the system to get closer to their goal. This can take years, if it happens at all. (7) Finally, if all the stars align, a player gets "called up" to the majors, where he strives to make the most of this rare opportunity.

*Ryan Bradley, pitching for the Richmond Flying Squirrels, a Double-A team of the San Francisco Giants, April 13, 2013*

**★ Text Marking ★**

Find the sequence of events.

☐ Box the signal words.

___ Underline the important events.

1-2-3 Number the events in the sequence they happen.

18 · *Informational Passages for Text Marking & Close Reading: Grade 5* · © 2015 by Scholastic Teaching Resources

---

# Passage 3: Path to the Bigs

**1.** C; Sample answer: After reading the article, I understand that players face a long, challenging path. For example, paragraph 4 describes the different minor league levels players must rise through.

**2.** B; Sample answer: In the first paragraph, the author writes that few people make it, and most don't.

**3.** Sample answer: I think the author is saying that the experience of playing in the major leagues is one that very, very few get to have. I think that "if all the stars align" means that everything has to go right at the same time for the player to reach his goal.

**4.** Sample answer: I think that because reaching the majors is so challenging and can take so long, the kind of person who would succeed must be patient, determined, competitive, tough, and, of course, super talented.

---

**4** Sequence of Events · Name _____ Date _____

## Reimbursement Request

**Read the business e-mail.
Then follow the directions in the Text Marking box.**

From: Susana Ramos<susana_ramos4307@gmail.com>
Sent: Tuesday, March 6, 2015
To: Kitty Kweezeen<comments@kittykweezeen.com>

Subject: Request for a refund

Dear Kitty Kweezeen:

For three years, I have been feeding my cat, (1) Stanley, various flavors of your brand of canned food. During that time, he would happily (2) devour whatever I served him and appeared vigorous, bright-eyed, and contented. But yesterday morning, everything changed. I attempted to serve him one of your new flavors: Feline Flambé. Since its principal ingredient is tuna—which Stanley adores—I thought he'd gobble it down. After (4) (3) I filled his bowl, he meowed plaintively, lay down, and later marched away hungry. He never once returned to Feline Flambé that day, which is NOT like Stanley. (5) So then I discarded all the Feline Flambé, scoured the bowl to remove any bits of food, and (6) served Stanley some of his old standby, your flavor called Kitty Konfetti. But he steadfastly refused (7) that, too. (8) Finally, I took Stanley to the vet. She confirmed that he is in fine health, so I've begun (9) feeding him a totally different brand of food that he seems to enjoy. Therefore, I respectfully (10) request a return of the $2.28 I spent on the four cans of Feline Flambé, serial number KK0691FF95, that unfortunately went to waste.

Thank you for your attention.

Yours truly,
Susana Ramos

**★ Text Marking ★**

Find the sequence of events.

☐ Box the signal words.

___ Underline the important events.

1-2-3 Number the events in the sequence they happened.

20 · *Informational Passages for Text Marking & Close Reading: Grade 5* · © 2015 by Scholastic Teaching Resources

---

# Passage 4: Reimbursement Request

**1.** C; Sample answer: *Reimbursement* is part of the title of the piece, and the subject line says, "Request for a *refund*." That's the reason the e-mail was written.

**2.** A; Sample answer: Susana only asks for a refund of the cost of the food, so she took Stanley to the vet to make sure there was no medical reason for him not eating.

**3.** Sample answer: The author wrote to complain about a kind of cat food her pet refused to eat and to request a refund for the money she spent on that food.

**4.** Sample answer: I can't know whether the company will send a refund, but I think that Susana explained the situation clearly, completely, and politely. She asked specifically for a refund to cover the wasted food, which sounds reasonable.

*Informational Passages for Text Marking & Close Reading: Grade 5*
© 2015 by Scholastic Teaching Resources

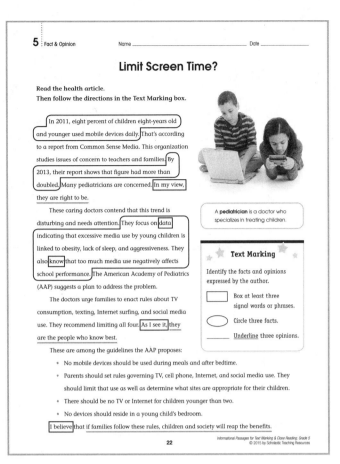

## Sample Text Markings

# Passage 5: Limit Screen Time?

**1.** C; Sample answer: It talks about a TV, and I know *viewing* is what you do when you watch TV.

**2.** D; Sample answer: Although families might spend too much on media, the article doesn't mention this as a problem.

**3.** Sample answer: Lists like this are easy to read. I think it helps make each guideline stand out from the others, and makes all the guidelines look like a group that belongs together.

**4.** Sample answer: If there is less use of media by young children, it may result in less obesity, better sleep, less aggressive behavior, and better school results. These changes would be very helpful.

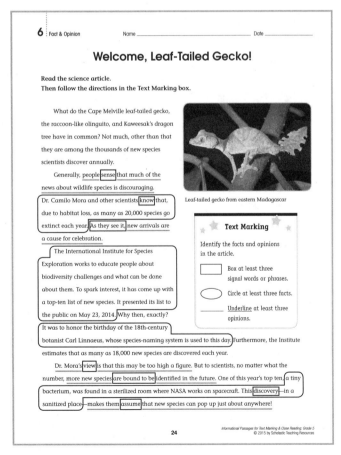

## Sample Text Markings

# Passage 6: Welcome, Leaf-Tailed Gecko!

**1.** C; Sample answer: The other choices are all synonyms for *sanitized*. Also, the last paragraph says that the room where it was found was sterilized, and I know that means very clean.

**2.** D; Sample answer: In paragraph 3, the author says "to spark interest" was the reason for this presentation.

**3.** Sample answer: The fact comes later in that paragraph—that as many as 20,000 species go extinct each year. We hear much more bad news than good news about wildlife species.

**4.** Sample answer: In the last paragraph, the author says that one of the top-ten species was a bacterium found in a sterilized place—exactly the kind of spot where you would think no new life could emerge. Scientists find this encouraging.

**56**

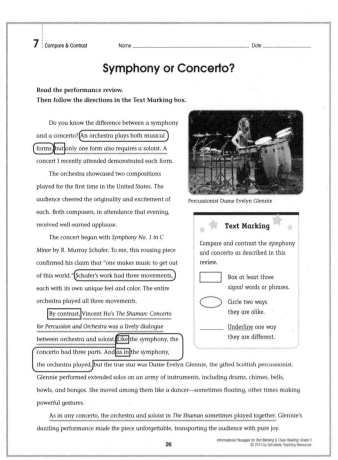

## Symphony or Concerto?

Read the performance review.
Then follow the directions in the Text Marking box.

Do you know the difference between a symphony and a concerto? An orchestra plays both musical forms, but only one form also requires a soloist. A concert I recently attended demonstrated each form.

The orchestra showcased two compositions played for the first time in the United States. The audience cheered the originality and excitement of each. Both composers, in attendance that evening, received well-earned applause.

The concert began with *Symphony No. 1 in C Minor* by R. Murray Schafer. To me, this rousing piece confirmed his claim that "one makes music to get out of this world." Schafer's work had three movements, each with its own unique feel and color. The entire orchestra played all three movements.

By contrast, Vincent Ho's *The Shaman: Concerto for Percussion and Orchestra* was a lively dialogue between orchestra and soloist. Like the symphony, the concerto had three parts. And as in the symphony, the orchestra played, but the true star was Dame Evelyn Glennie, the gifted Scottish percussionist. Glennie performed extended solos on an army of instruments, including drums, chimes, bells, bowls, and bongos. She moved among them like a dancer—sometimes floating, other times making powerful gestures.

As in any concerto, the orchestra and soloist in *The Shaman* sometimes played together. Glennie's dazzling performance made the piece unforgettable, transporting the audience with pure joy.

Percussionist Dame Evelyn Glennie

### ★ Text Marking ★

Compare and contrast the symphony and concerto as described in this review.

☐ Box at least three signal words or phrases.

◯ Circle two ways they are alike.

___ Underline one way they are different.

26

*Informational Passages for Text Marking & Close Reading: Grade 5*
© 2015 by Scholastic Teaching Resources

---

◀ Sample Text Markings

## Passage 7: Symphony or Concerto?

**1.** B; Sample answer: In paragraph 4, the author used the word *parts* to talk about the concerto. So I figured that movements are parts of longer pieces of music.

**2.** C; The author gives information of interest to people who like concerts, but it would be too challenging for people with no background information and not detailed enough for music scholars.

**3.** Sample answer: The author liked the concert very much and was especially delighted by the wonderful performance given by soloist Dame Evelyn Glennie.

**4.** Sample answer: A symphony and a concerto are both musical forms. Both involve an orchestra. The symphony and concerto the reviewer heard were both played in the United States for the first time and each had three parts. But a concerto is written for an orchestra and a soloist, while a symphony is written only for orchestra.

---

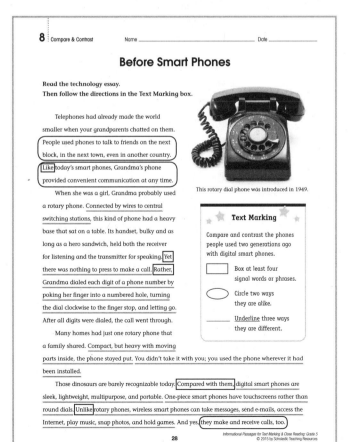

## Before Smart Phones

Read the technology essay.
Then follow the directions in the Text Marking box.

Telephones had already made the world smaller when your grandparents chatted on them. People used phones to talk to friends on the next block, in the next town, even in another country. Like today's smart phones, Grandma's phone provided convenient communication at any time.

When she was a girl, Grandma probably used a rotary phone. Connected by wires to central switching stations, this kind of phone had a heavy base that sat on a table. Its handset, bulky and as long as a hero sandwich, held both the receiver for listening and the transmitter for speaking. Yet there was nothing to press to make a call. Rather, Grandma dialed each digit of a phone number by poking her finger into a numbered hole, turning the dial clockwise to the finger stop, and letting go. After all digits were dialed, the call went through.

Many homes had just one rotary phone that a family shared. Compact, but heavy with moving parts inside, the phone stayed put. You didn't take it with you; you used the phone wherever it had been installed.

Those dinosaurs are barely recognizable today. Compared with them, digital smart phones are sleek, lightweight, multipurpose, and portable. One-piece smart phones have touchscreens rather than round dials. Unlike rotary phones, wireless smart phones can take messages, send e-mails, access the Internet, play music, snap photos, and hold games. And yes, they make and receive calls, too.

This rotary dial phone was introduced in 1949.

### ★ Text Marking ★

Compare and contrast the phones people used two generations ago with digital smart phones.

☐ Box at least four signal words or phrases.

◯ Circle two ways they are alike.

___ Underline three ways they are different.

28

*Informational Passages for Text Marking & Close Reading: Grade 5*
© 2015 by Scholastic Teaching Resources

---

◀ Sample Text Markings

## Passage 8: Before Smart Phones

**1.** B; Sample answer: The photo helped me visualize the rotary dial, which is round and turns, which is like a rotation.

**2.** C; At the end paragraph 1, the author says that Grandma's phone provided convenient communication and that smart phones do, too.

**3.** Sample answer: The physical size of the world is the same as it always was, but the telephone allowed communicating across distances, making people feel more closely connected and nearby, even if they really weren't.

**4.** Sample answer: Rotary phones were heavy, connected by wires, and could only receive and transmit voice calls. Smart phones can make and receive calls, too, but can also do many other tasks, and are sleek, lightweight, wireless, one-piece, and portable.

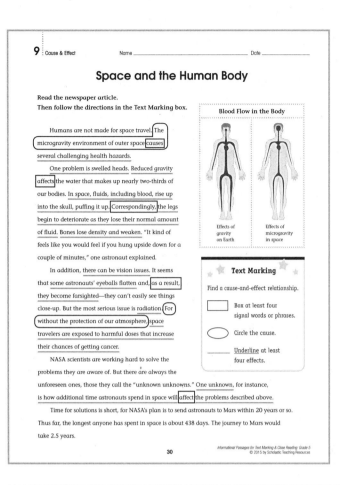

## Passage 9: Space and the Human Body

**1.** B; Sample answer: In paragraph 3, the article explains that someone who is farsighted has trouble seeing things close-up.

**2.** A; Sample answer: The other three choices were clearly stated in the article.

**3.** Sample answer: The illustration contrasts the normal distribution of blood in the human body with the change that happens in microgravity. You can see that the figure on the right has much less blood going to his legs and arms, and more than normal in the head.

**4.** Sample answer: I think the author includes this fact to remind readers that such a journey will expose astronauts to all of the problems mentioned, plus any "unknown unknowns" that might arise due to extended time in space.

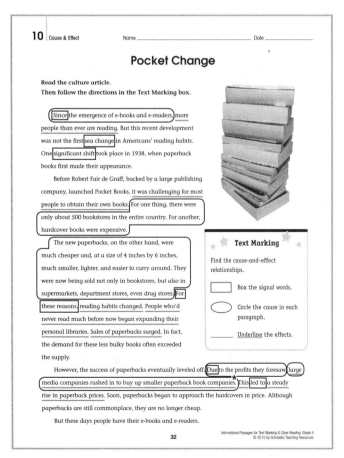

## Passage 10: Pocket Change

**1.** C; Sample answer: In the first paragraph, the author writes "more people than ever are reading."

**2.** B; Sample answer: All of the other choices are true according to the article. Knowing how to read wasn't discussed in the article.

**3.** Sample answer: I think the author is describing a significant change, a major one that is very noticeable.

**4.** Sample answer: Because both were cheaper, more easily available, and smaller than hardcover books, more people than ever could easily get reading material.

\* The phrase in the passage that is circled and underlined is both a cause and an effect.

## Bigger Than Big

Read the word origin article.
Then follow the directions in the Text Marking box.

As any cook or farmer can confirm, "jumbo" eggs are much bigger than large eggs. The biggest jets in a fleet are nicknamed "jumbo" jets. Most people use the word *jumbo* to describe anything bigger than usual. But how did this now-common adjective get its start?

Some English speakers link the term *jumbo* to a famous African pachyderm by that name. That elephant lives on to this day, thanks to the fame it earned as part of P.T. Barnum's "Greatest Show on Earth." The original Jumbo was captured by an African hunting party in 1861. At the time, this 13,000-pound behemoth was one of the largest elephants ever seen in that part of the world. The locals called him Jumbo—an English spelling of the Swahili word for chief.

Jumbo was sent to a zoo in Paris, and later transferred to a London zoo. But he was a cantankerous captive. The keeper worried that Jumbo's grouchy and unpredictable behavior might make him too dangerous for a zoo. So the grand tusker was sold to P.T. Barnum, who featured him to amaze circus audiences.

Or so the origin story goes…

Another conjecture about the roots of *jumbo* traces the word to a London zookeeper. This notion states that *jumbo* was based on the Zulu word *jumba*, which means a large parcel. No matter the theory, there's no question that Jumbo certainly was enormous!

Jumbo the elephant in the 1880s

### ★ Text Marking ★

Use context clues to unlock word meanings.

◯   Circle the words *cantankerous* and *conjecture*.

____   Underline context clues for each word.

34

*Informational Passages for Text Marking & Close Reading: Grade 5*
© 2015 by Scholastic Teaching Resources

◀ Sample Text Markings

## Passage 11: Bigger Than Big

**1**. C; Sample answer: In paragraph 3, the article says that the zoo feared that Jumbo might be too dangerous to keep.

**2**. D; Sample answer: I read each pair to find the one with two synonyms. Context clues in the last paragraph helped me know that the words in D both mean the same thing.

**3**. Sample answer: The word *pachyderm* is followed by the words "that elephant," so I figured out that a pachyderm is an elephant.

**4**. Sample answer: I think the author wanted to give common examples that most of us know before going on to tell the story of the giant elephant whose name became an adjective.

---

## The Shadow Catcher

Read the sociology essay.
Then follow the directions in the Text Marking box.

His goal was to live among Native Americans and document their traditional ways of life. That was a formidable and perilous undertaking in 1900. But when Seattle-based photographer Edward Curtis finally completed this epic project, it was hailed by the *New York Herald* as "…the most ambitious enterprise in publishing since…the King James Bible."

Curtis essentially left behind a successful photography business to pursue his dream. With support from President Theodore Roosevelt and funds from the wealthy J. P. Morgan, he eagerly began his quest. He packed his photography and recording equipment, gathered supplies, assistants, and interpreters, and ventured into Indian territories. Rugged terrain, illness, intense heat, freezing temperatures, and suspicious native groups did not deter him. Determined to capture lifestyles that he knew would soon vanish, Curtis persevered. The results were astonishing.

From the Inuit of the far north to the Havasupai within the depths of the Grand Canyon, Curtis visited more than 80 tribes. Over 30 years, he took 40,000 photos and collected 10,000 audio recordings of music and language. Notable leaders like Geronimo, Red Cloud, and Chief Joseph posed for him. He got on well with his subjects. They called him the Shadow Catcher.

Curtis's finished work amounted to 20 volumes of pictures and text. His remarkable achievement is the most definitive archive of American Indian life. It remains a priceless cultural treasure.

Curtis took this photo of family members from the Piegan tribe in 1910.

### ★ Text Marking ★

Use context clues to unlock word meanings.

◯   Circle the words *perilous* and *capture*.

____   Underline context clues for each word.

36

*Informational Passages for Text Marking & Close Reading: Grade 5*
© 2015 by Scholastic Teaching Resources

◀ Sample Text Markings

## Passage 12: The Shadow Catcher

**1**. B; Sample answer: In paragraph 2, I read about the different dangers Curtis faced on his journey.

**2**. D; Sample answer: The author is discussing the photography and recordings Curtis collected to make a record of Indian life before it was too late. These things are documents so D seemed like the best answer.

**3**. Sample answers: It was a difficult, dangerous, and expensive pursuit that required a lot of equipment; Curtis gave up a business to follow a dream; the results were amazing and are still valuable today because they show us a way of life that no longer exists.

**4**. Sample answer: I think that *persevered* means to be determined to carry on, even in the face of dangers and hardships.

*Informational Passages for Text Marking & Close Reading: Grade 5*
© 2015 by Scholastic Teaching Resources

## A Worldwide Pickle

Read the nutrition article.
Then follow the directions in the Text Marking box.

Nature demands that living things must eat to survive. This might seem easy in a modern world of freezers, supermarkets, and restaurants. But in the past, the problem was that much food spoiled before anyone could eat it. Our ancestors knew that without food, they would die. So they needed to find ways to treat foods to make them last. They had to preserve enough food in good times to survive harsh winters, droughts, natural disasters, and seasonal shortages.

One early answer to making food last was *pickling*. Pickling is a way to preserve foods by curing them in vinegar and/or salt to prevent spoiling. Vinegar is an acid that kills most bacteria. Salt dries food out and aids in the growth of "good" bacteria that protect against the "bad" bacteria that cause rot. Nearly every culture in the world developed pickled foods.

Science has since proven that pickling not only makes food last longer, it also makes some of it easier to digest. In fact, certain foods become more nutritious after they have been pickled. Pickling can also convert inedible foods, such as some roots or plants, into healthy new forms.

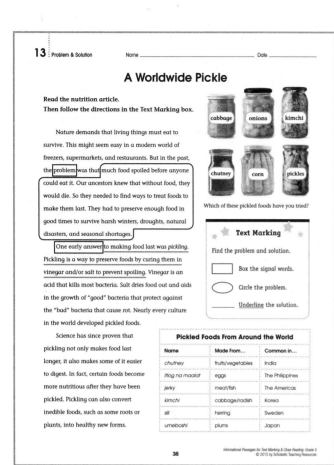
cabbage | onions | kimchi
chutney | corn | pickles

Which of these pickled foods have you tried?

⭐ **Text Marking** ⭐

Find the problem and solution.

☐ Box the signal words.

◯ Circle the problem.

___ Underline the solution.

**Pickled Foods From Around the World**

| Name | Made From... | Common in... |
|---|---|---|
| chutney | fruits/vegetables | India |
| itlog na maalat | eggs | The Philippines |
| jerky | meat/fish | The Americas |
| kimchi | cabbage/radish | Korea |
| sill | herring | Sweden |
| umeboshi | plums | Japan |

◀ Sample Text Markings

## Passage 13: A Worldwide Pickle

**1.** A; Sample answer: The end of the article talks about converting inedible foods into healthy foods, so I assume they are changing things we couldn't eat into things we can. Also, I know that the prefix *in-* means "not," and *edible* means you can eat it.

**2.** D; Sample answer: I know that pork is a kid of meat, and salting it would help it last longer. I don't think that vinegar or salt would make the other choices last longer—or taste good to eat!

**3.** Sample answer: I think the author wants to show that foods are pickled in all cultures of the world. The chart offers a look at some of them.

**4.** Sample answer: Preserving food has been a challenge throughout history, and another meaning of the word *pickle* is a problem or bad situation. So, "worldwide pickle" refers to the method of preserving food done all around the world, and also suggests the problem itself.

---

## Space Junk

Read the environment essay.
Then follow the directions in the Text Marking box.

All countries that send objects into space confront a serious problem: space junk. The "junk" consists of parts of rockets, debris from launches, dead satellites, and other manufactured items afloat in space. There may well be half a million pieces of dangerous waste in orbit. As you might expect, countries around the world are concerned. Many are working on solutions to destroy the detritus.

Japan's space agency has built an electromagnetic tether. This giant steel and aluminum net, nearly half a mile wide, would orbit in space and attract metallic fragments as it travels. Once full of waste, the net would fall back into the Earth's atmosphere. The gathered fragments would burn upon re-entry. If this net idea works, Japan intends to build a much larger one.

A Swiss company proposes a different answer. It is developing a spacecraft that would act as a huge catcher's mitt to snatch harmful debris. Like the Japanese net, the Swiss "glove" would fall back into Earth's atmosphere, destroying its contents in the process.

Not surprisingly, scientists in the United States are also seeking solutions to the challenge of hazardous space rubble. One team's curious proposal may provide the most captivating resolution—and would save on fuel, too. Its plan is to build what it calls the Space Sweeper with Sling-Sat. Acting like a gigantic sling-shot, this gizmo would capture objects and fling them toward the Earth's atmosphere.

Illustration of space debris destroying part of a satellite

⭐ **Text Marking** ⭐

Find the problem and solutions.

☐ Box the signal words.

◯ Circle the problem.

___ Underline the solutions.

◀ Sample Text Markings

## Passage 14: Space Junk

**1.** B; Sample answer: The details in the paragraph helped me know that *detritus* is another word for waste or junk.

**2.** D; Sample answer: The essay doesn't discuss cost or readiness. The other inventions might have names though they are not given. D is specifically mentioned in the last paragraph.

**3.** Sample answer: Both ideas rely on something to catch the junk and bring it back into Earth's atmosphere where it will burn up.

**4.** Sample answer: I think that the nations are concerned that orbiting space junk can be dangerous to astronauts, satellites, space stations, and other kinds of orbiting equipment used in space programs and communications. Plus, the illustration shows space junk destroying a satellite.

## "Creative Elegance"

**Read the fine arts essay.**
**Then follow the directions in the Text Marking box.**

"My journey begins with the line," states Salma Arastu. In her art, Arastu uses looping, continuous lines to suggest her hope for a world united in peace. Professor Richard Viera of Lehigh University wrote that her art "…reflects, as well as transcends, all barriers with compassion and creative elegance." I resolved to learn more about this California-based Hindu-Muslim painter, sculptor, and poet.

Artist Salma Arastu at work on a painting

Born in India in 1950, Salma Arastu was the tenth and youngest child in her family. Due to a birth defect, she had no fingers on her left hand. Her mother helped her view this challenge as a blessing, and encouraged Salma to seek her purpose in life. Salma began drawing loops and curves and never stopped. Art helped her explore, accept, and embrace the world in all its variations. She says that her art attempts to "build bridges between all faiths and form a dialogue of understanding."

★ **Text Marking** ★

Summarize the text.

◯ Circle the topic.

＿＿＿ Underline important details.

I visited The Triton Museum of Art in Santa Clara to see her one-woman show. There, I also learned that she does digital art and has written and illustrated greeting cards and books of poetry.

Arastu's graceful paintings moved me deeply. I believe that she is one of the finest artists working today. Her canvases are both alive and soothingly peaceful. In some, she paints lacy Arabic calligraphy atop softly colored backgrounds. Even without knowing the meanings of the words, the sheer beauty inspired me.

42

◀ Sample Text Markings

## Passage 15: "Creative Elegance"

**1**. C; Sample answer: The essay discusses Arastu's lifelong interest in using art to bring people together despite their differences.

**2**. D; Sample answer: Paragraph 2 describes how her mother helped Salma view her birth defect as a blessing and encouraged her to seek her purpose in life.

**3**. Sample answer: Hindu-Muslim artist Salma Arastu strives to use her art to build bridges among different people, cultures, and ideas. She never let her own difference stop her from exploring ways that bring people together instead of divide them. As a painter, sculptor, and poet, she seeks to inspire peace.

**4**. Sample answer: In paragraph 4, it is the author's opinion that Arastu is "one of the finest artists working today." The beauty of Arastu's art has inspired the author. But these are personal views, not facts.

---

## Animal Weather Forecasters?

**Read the magazine article.**
**Then follow the directions in the Text Marking box.**

Will earthworms wriggle out of the ground prior to a flood? Will sharks swim to deeper waters before a hurricane? Do animals actually have powers beyond those that guide them in their daily lives, powers that enable them to predict natural disasters like earthquakes or hurricanes? The short answer is probably "No." But the long answer is more complex.

Scientists are skeptical that animals have a special sense that enables them to predict the weather. But they know that many animals have more highly developed senses than humans do, and are capable of detecting signals of impending weather change sooner than we can. Some, like dogs, pick up infrasonic sound waves—sounds that are at lower frequencies than we can hear. Others, like the frogs that go silent before a storm, can detect differences in air pressure. However they get their signals, animals learn to associate them with danger. Those signals alert them that it is time to move to a safer area.

Changes in air pressure may cause seagulls to seek shelter on land.

★ **Text Marking** ★

Summarize the text.

◯ Circle the topic.

＿＿＿ Underline important details.

All animals have a strong survival instinct, but can they predict weather patterns? Does a groundhog know what kind of spring lies ahead? Will a black bear choose its winter den depending on how cold the upcoming winter promises to be? Not likely, say the scientists. But if you spot a cluster of birds hunkering down outside your window, you'd be wise to take your umbrella.

44

◀ Sample Text Markings

## Passage 16: Animal Weather Forecasters?

**1**. D; Sample answer: The article says that animals can detect change in weather before it happens, so I guessed that *impending* means approaching, or coming.

**2**. B; Sample answer: The article mentions each of the other choices but it says in the last paragraph that it's not likely that animals can predict weather patterns.

**3**. Sample answer: The article explores whether animals can predict natural disasters. Scientists are skeptical of this, but they do acknowledge that animals have superior senses that help them sense weather changes before humans can.

**4**. Sample answer: I think the author recognizes that, as appealing as it might be to link animal behavior with the power to predict disasters, scientists do not strongly support this idea. There are some apparent connections, but no actual proof of extraordinary powers has been found.

## Passage 17 worksheet

**17** Make Inferences        Name _____        Date _____

### ¡Si, Se Pueda!

**Read the biographical sketch.**
**Then follow the directions in the Text Marking box.**

"We draw our strength from the very despair in which we have been forced to live," said activist Cesar Chavez. And he knew what he was talking about.

Chavez was born in Arizona in 1927 to immigrant parents. They owned a small farm and lived in an adobe house built by his grandfather. Soon, hard times forced his family to relocate to California, where they moved from farm to farm picking crops. Chavez understood firsthand the tough lives migrant workers led. Hardened by his experiences, he dedicated himself to improving those wretched conditions.

Migrant workers had it rough. Their camps were unsanitary. Their labor was long and backbreaking and the pay meager. In addition, the migrants faced bitter prejudice. Chavez began his work for change.

Drawing on what he observed in the civil rights movement, he organized the powerless workers to fight the powerful growers nonviolently. Chavez organized protest marches, boycotts, and hunger strikes. Through his dogged efforts—including a lengthy hunger strike of his own—and against great odds, Chavez accomplished many of his goals. He died in 1993, a hero who left America a better place than he found it.

During his courageous efforts to win improvements for migrant workers, Cesar Chavez coined the phrase *¡Si, se pueda!* which means "Yes, it can be done!" This inspiring slogan still rings true today.

Cesar Chavez speaking to migrant workers in 1985

> ★ **Text Marking** ★
>
> Make an inference: What is an activist?
>
> _____ Underline text clues.
>
> 💡 Think about what you already know.

46

*Informational Passages for Text Marking & Close Reading: Grade 5*
© 2015 by Scholastic Teaching Resources

---

◀ Sample Text Markings

## Passage 17: *¡Si, Se Pueda!*

**1**. B; Sample answer: Paragraph 1 begins with a quotation by Chavez that is summarized in choice B.

**2**. C; Sample answer: A person has to be persistent to go on a hunger strike and to organize an entire group of people to work for change.

**3**. Sample answer: I think an activist is someone like Cesar Chavez. He was a man who decided to become active in working for change and devoted himself to a cause, no matter the odds or the challenges.

**4**. Sample answer: I think that a migrant worker is a person who moves around from farm to farm picking crops. A migrant worker may live in poor conditions and earn low wages.

---

**18** Make Inferences        Name _____        Date _____

### Malala Day

**Read the blog post.**
**Then follow the directions in the Text Marking box.**

On July 12, 2013, the United Nations honored an innocent Pakistani teen whose near-death focused worldwide attention on the need for education. "Malala Day" was held to pay tribute to Malala Yousafzai. When she was fifteen, extremists opposing education for girls attempted to kill her. Though gravely wounded, Malala recovered to become a courageous champion for the rights of millions of girls worldwide whose gender denies them a chance at an education.

It was Malala's sixteenth birthday that day, and my eleventh. She quietly and modestly addressed hundreds of people in her first public speech since the cruel attack on her the October before. She never voiced anger, nor did she call for revenge. She spoke passionately about her goals for education, equality, and peace. One sentence she uttered that day became a slogan: *One child, one teacher, one pen, and one book can change the world.*

Malala Yousafzai gently but firmly denounced terrorism and urged greater respect and dignity for all people. Listening to her speech online gave me goosebumps and brought tears to my eyes. She seemed so mature and peaceful, yet she's the same age as my sister. It made me realize how powerful one girl, a deeply-held belief, and thoughtful words can be. She is a model to me of bravery, self-esteem, and hope.

Malala Yousafzai speaking at the United Nations

> In 2014, Malala was awarded the Nobel Peace Prize, the youngest person ever to win this honor.

> ★ **Text Marking** ★
>
> Make an inference: What sort of person is Malala Yousafzai?
>
> _____ Underline text clues.
>
> 💡 Think about what you already know.

48

*Informational Passages for Text Marking & Close Reading: Grade 5*
© 2015 by Scholastic Teaching Resources

---

◀ Sample Text Markings

## Passage 18: Malala Day

**1**. D; Sample answer: This title most accurately represents the main ideas of the blog post.

**2**. A; Sample answer: The exact words Malala spoke that day were so clear, to the point, and inspiring that they become a motto for her cause.

**3**. Sample answer: Malala strongly favors peace, equality, education, and respect. Wanting revenge isn't always thought through. She was a victim of violence, so I infer that she probably wouldn't want to be any part of more violence to others.

**4**. Sample answer: Despite the attack on Malala, she found the courage to speak out for education, human rights, and dignity. So I infer that she is a sensitive, intelligent, strong-willed, mature, caring person who hopes to use her personal story to inspire others to join her in making the world a better place.

## Food Without a Face

Read the business letter.
Then follow the directions in the Text Marking box.

Veggie wraps

To Principal Fergerson:

(P)  I respectfully request that you and our cafeteria staff rethink the lunch program. My Buddhist family follows a vegetarian diet. (I) We believe that animals are living beings that we should not kill and eat for food. My dad says, (I) "Don't eat anything with a face." This may sound strange to you. However, it helps us remember to avoid eating beef, lamb, pork, goat, chicken, turkey, and fish.

 Our daily school lunches almost always offer some kind of meat, such as hot dogs, burgers, chicken, or fish (I) sticks. I cannot eat any of these foods without violating my beliefs. I do not expect all meals to be vegetarian, since I (P) realize that not all students believe as I do. But I'd find it much easier if the menu included meatless choices.

 Do consider adding simple options for me and my brother Kai, and others I know who wish or need to forgo (P) meat. Please provide sliced cheeses or peanut butter for sandwiches, hard-boiled eggs, yogurt, hummus, or veggie wraps. Why not serve fresh salad with meatless add-ons, like nuts, cheese, avocado, lentils, bean sprouts, or tofu? That would surely appeal to many students and teachers, including those who do eat meat.

(P)  Thanks for considering my request. My parents say they'll happily offer some easy, kid-friendly ideas.
Yours truly,
Charini Anzan
Mr. Delgado's Grade 5 class

**Text Marking**

Check to identify the author's two purposes.

☐ to entertain (E)
☑ to inform (I)
☑ to persuade (P)

_____ Underline text clues for this purpose. Write E, I, or P in the margin beside each clue.

50

*Informational Passages for Text Marking & Close Reading: Grade 5*
© 2015 by Scholastic Teaching Resources

◀ Sample Text Markings

## Passage 19: Food Without a Face

**1.** A; Sample answer: I reread the paragraph with that word and understood from the context that *violating* means going against or breaking a rule. A is the only choice that involves eating meat, so it's the best answer.

**2.** D; In paragraph 1, the author discusses her family's vegetarianism, and in paragraph 2, she says she cannot eat at the school cafeteria without going against her beliefs.

**3.** Sample answer: I think Charini must be someone who tries to accept the views of others, even if they differ from her own. She doesn't ask for a ban on meat in the cafeteria. She also notes in paragraph 3 that even those who do eat meat might still enjoy some vegetarian options. Her letter also makes her seem smart and reasonable.

**4.** Sample answer: Charini requests that the school cafeteria provide vegetarian choices for her and others who either also follow a vegetarian diet, or who might enjoy vegetarian choices from time to time. She offers reasons for her stance and suggestions for meeting her request.

## He Did All That?

Read the history essay.
Then follow the directions in the Text Marking box.

Benjamin Franklin playing his glass armonica

 Diplomat, philosopher, and businessman, Benjamin Franklin was the foremost American of his day. He was a pivotal figure in colonial and revolutionary times, and the architect of an alliance with France that ensured the colonies' independence from England. A much-admired (I) figure in politics, this legendary American was a scientific and engineering genius, too.

 The list and breadth of his inventions are astonishing. Let's start with electricity, which Franklin did not invent. But he did grasp its properties, coining several terms, such as *battery*, *charge*, and *conductor*, in the process. (I) He applied his understanding to invent the lightning rod, a metal device that protected houses from the "mischief" of lightning.

 Franklin could not see clearly up close. When he (I) invented bifocals—glasses with distinct upper and lower halves, one for distance, one for reading—he had his own condition in mind. To advance his love for swimming, (I) he built fins that attached to the hands. And when he noticed, after eight transatlantic crossings, that speed was (I) affected by the Gulf Stream, he mapped that critical coastal current.

 Then there was the Franklin stove. This iron structure provided better airflow and longer-lasting (I) heat than a fireplace did. (I) He also designed the glass armonica, a musical instrument made of glass bowls color-coded by note. And he built an odometer to record the distance carriage wheels traveled. (I)

 Where did he get the time?

**Text Marking**

Check to identify the author's purpose.

☐ to entertain (E)
☑ to inform (I)
☐ to persuade (P)

_____ Underline text clues for each purpose. Write E, I, or P in the margin beside each clue.

52

*Informational Passages for Text Marking & Close Reading: Grade 5*
© 2015 by Scholastic Teaching Resources

◀ Sample Text Markings

## Passage 20: He Did All That?

**1.** B; Sample answer: Paragraph 1 describes Franklin as the foremost American of his day, and goes on to mention some of his important political achievements.

**2.** D; Sample answer: After reading about Franklin's many inventions, I also wondered where he found the time to do everything he did! It also relates back to the title of the essay to make a clever ending.

**3.** Sample answer: It was probably Franklin's own word describing the kind of trouble lightning could cause.

**4.** Sample answer: The author mainly focuses on the non-political contributions Ben Franklin made to American life by describing some of his many inventions and innovations. The author probably hopes to bring attention to the lesser known but still amazing achievements.

# Notes

*Informational Passages for Text Marking & Close Reading: Grade 5*
© 2015 by Scholastic Teaching Resources